M000072924

WITH CHRIST IN THE SCHOOL OF PRAYER

By Andrew Murray

Copyright 2019 by Blessed News Publishing

CONTENTS

ILLUSTRATIONS...5

PREFACE 17

CHAPTER 1: Lord, teach us to pray or The Only Teacher 21

CHAPTER 2: In Spirit and truth OR The True Worshippers 29

CHAPTER 3: Pray to thy Father, Which is in Secret OR Alone with God 35

CHAPTER 4: After this manner pray or The Model Prayer................ 43

CHAPTER 5: Ask and It Shall be Given You or The Certainty of the Answer to Prayer.. 51

CHAPTER 6: How much more? ' or The Infinite Fatherliness of God 59

CHAPTER 7: How much more the Holy Spirit OR The All Comprehensive Gift... 65

CHAPTER 8: Because of his Importunity or The Boldness of God's Friends... 71

CHAPTER 9: Prayer Provides Laborers.. 79

CHAPTER 10: Prayer Must Be Specific.. 85

CHAPTER 11: The Faith That Takes... 91

CHAPTER 12: The Secret of Believing Prayer 99

CHAPTER 13: Prayer and Fasting... 107

CHAPTER 14: Prayer and Love 115

CHAPTER 15: The Power of United Prayer.................................. 121

CHAPTER 16: The Power of Persevering Prayer.......................... 129

CHAPTER 17: Prayer in Harmony with God 137

CHAPTER 18: Prayer in Harmony with the Destiny of Man.......... 143

CHAPTER 19: Power for Praying and Working 151

CHAPTER 20: The Chief End of Prayer..159

CHAPTER 21: The All-Inclusive Condition..165

CHAPTER 22: The Word and Prayer..173

CHAPTER 23: Obedience: The Path to Power in Prayer....................181

CHAPTER 24: The All-Powerful Plea..189

CHAPTER 25: The Holy Spirit and Prayer..197

CHAPTER 26: Christ the Intercessor 205

CHAPTER 27: Christ the High Priest 213

CHAPTER 28: Christ the Sacrifice..221

CHAPTER 29: Our Boldness in Prayer..229

CHAPTER 30: The Ministry of Intercession..239

CHAPTER 31: A Life of Prayer 247

ILLUSTRATIONS

Photograph of Andrew Murray

Christ by Jose Benlliure y Gil

Baptism of Christ by Jose de Ribera

Ecce Homo by Caravaggio

Prayings Hands by Durer

The Andrew Murray House in South Africa Courtesy of Carla de Villiers

St Francis in Prayer by Caravaggio

The Andrew Murray Memorial in Wellington Courtesy of A3alb

The Angelus by Jean Francois Millet

The Deposition of Christ by Raffaello

The Four Evangelists by Jacob Jordaens

The Raising of Lazarus by Rembrandt

PREFACE

O F ALL THE PROMISES CONNECTED WITH THE COMMAND, ABIDE IN ME,' there is none higher, and none that sooner brings the confession, 'Not that I have already attained, or am already made perfect,' than this: 'If ye abide in me, ask whatsoever ye will, and it shall be done unto you.' Power with God is the highest attainment of the life of full abiding.

And of all the traits of a life like CHRIST there is none higher and more glorious than conformity to Him in the work that now engages Him without ceasing in the Father's presence-His all-prevailing intercession. The more we abide in Him, and grow unto His likeness, will His priestly life work in us mightily, and our life become what His is, a life that ever pleads and prevails for men.

Thou hast made us kings and priests unto God. Both in the king and the priest the chief thing is power, influence, blessing. In the king it is the power coming downward; in the priest the power rising upward, prevailing with God. In our blessed Priest-King, Jesus Christ, the kingly power is founded on the priestly 'He is able to save to the uttermost, because He ever liveth to make intercession.' in us, His priests and kings, it is no otherwise: it is in intercession that the Church is to find and wield its highest power, that each member ofthe, Church is to prove his descent from Israel, who as a prince had power with God and with men, and prevailed

It is under a deep impression that the place and power of prayer in the Christian life is too little understood that this book has been written. I feel sure that as long as we look on prayer chiefly as the means of maintaining our own Christian life, we shall not know fully what it is meant to be. But when we learn to regard it as the highest part of the work entrusted to us, the root and strength of all other work, we shall see that there is nothing that we so need to study and practice as the art of praying aright. If I have at all succeeded in pointing out the progressive teaching of our Lord in regard to prayer and the distinct reference the wonderful promises , of the last night (John 16:16) have to the works we are to do in His name, to the greater works, and to the bearing much fruit, we shall all admit that it is only when the Church gives herself up to this holy work of intercession that we can expect the power of Christ to manifest itself in her behalf. It is my prayer that God may use this little book to make clearer to some of His children the wonderful place of power and influence which He is waiting for them to occupy, and for which a weary world is waiting too.

In connection with this there is another truth that has come to me with wonderful clearness as I studied the teaching of Jesus on prayer. It is this: that the Father waits to hear every prayer of faith,: to give us whatsoever we will and whatsoever we ask in Jesus' name. We have become so accustomed to limit the wonderful love and the large promises of our God, that we cannot read the simplest and clearest statements of our Lord without the qualifying clauses by which we guard and expound them. If there is one thing I think the Church needs to learn, it is that God means prayer to have an answer, and that it hath not entered into the heart of man to conceive what God will do for His child who gives himself to believe that his prayer will be heard. God hears prayer; this is a truth universally admitted, but of which very few understand the meaning, or experience the power. If what I have written stirs my reader to go to the Master's words, and take His wondrous promises simply and literally as they stand, my object has been attained.

And then just one thing more. Thousands have in these last years found an unspeakable blessing in learning how completely Christ is our life, and how He undertakes to be and to do all in us that we need. I know not if we have yet learned to apply this truth to our prayerlife. Many complain that they have not the power to pray in faith, to pray the effectual prayer that availeth much. The message I would fain bring them is that the blessed Jesus is waiting, is longing, to teach them this. Christ is our life: in heaven He ever liveth to pray; His life in us is an ever-praying life, if we will but trust Him for it. Christ teaches us to pray not only by example, by instruction, by command, by promises, but by showing us HIMSELF the ever-living Intercessor, as our Life. It is when we believe this, and go and abide in Him for our prayer-life too, that our fears of not being able to pray aright will vanish, and we shall joyfully and triumphantly trust our Lord to teach us to pray, to be Himself the life and the power of our prayer.

May God open our eyes to see what the holy ministry of intercession is, to which, as His royal priesthood, we have been set apart. May He give us a large and strong heart to believe what mighty influence our prayers can exert. And may all fear as to our being able to fulfil our vocation vanish as we see Jesus, living ever to pray, living and standing surety for our prayer-life.

ANDREW MURRAY

CHAPTER 1:
LORD, TEACH US TO PRAY
OR THE ONLY TEACHER

And it came to pass, as He was praying in a certain place,
that when He ceased, one of His disciples said to Him, Lord,
teach us to pray. - Luke 11:1

THE DISCIPLES HAD BEEN WITH CHRIST, AND SEEN HIM pray. They had learnt to understand something of the connection between His wondrous life in public, and His secret life of prayer. They had learnt to believe in Him as a Master in the art of prayer-none could pray like Him. And so they came to Him with the request, 'Lord, teach us to pray.' And in after years they would have told us that there were few things more wonderful or blessed that He taught them than His lessons on prayer.

And now still it comes to pass, as He is praying in a certain place, that disciples who see Him thus engaged feel the need of repeating the same request, 'Lord, teach us to pray.' As we grow in the Christian life, the thought and the faith of the Beloved Master in His never-failing intercession becomes ever more precious, and the hope of being Like Christ in His intercession gains an attractiveness before unknown. And as we see Him pray, and remember that there is none who can pray like Him, and none who can teach like Him, we feel the petition of the disciples, `Lord, teach us to pray,' is just what we need. And as we think how all He is and has, how He Himself is our very own, how He is Himself our life, we feel assured that we have but to ask, and He will be delighted to take us up into closer fellowship with Himself, and teach us to pray even as He prays.

Come, my brothers! Shall we not go to the Blessed Master and ask Him to enroll our names too anew in that school which He always keeps open for those who long to continue their studies in the Divine art of prayer and intercession? Yes, let us this very day say to the Master, as they did of old `Lord, teach us to pray.' As we meditate we shall find each word of the petition we bring to be full of meaning.

'Lord, teach us to pray.' Yes, to pray. This is what we need to be taught. Though in its beginnings prayer is so simple that the feeblest child can pray, yet it is at the same time the highest and holiest work to which man can rise. It is fellowship with the Unseen and Most Holy One. The powers of the eternal world have been placed at its disposal. It is the very essence of true religion the channel of all blessings, the secret of power and life. Not only for ourselves, but for others, for the Church for the world, it is to prayer that God has given the right to take hold of Him and His strength. It is on prayer that the promises wait for their fulfilment the kingdom for its coming, the glory of God for its full revelation. And for this blessed work, how slothful and unfit we are. It is only the Spirit of God can enable us to do it aright. How speedily we are deceived into a resting in the form, while the power is wanting. Our early training, the teaching of the Church, the influence , of habit, the stirring of the emotions-how easily these lead to prayer which has no Spiritual power, and avails but little. True prayer, -that takes hold of God's strength; 'that availeth much, to which the gates of heaven are really opened wide-who would not cry, Oh for some one to teach me thus to pray?

Jesus has opened a school, in which He trains His redeemed ones, who specially desire it, to have power in prayer. Shall we not enter it with the petition, Lord! it is just this we need to be taught! O teach us to pray.

'Lord, teach us to pray.' Yes, us, Lord. We have read in Thy Word with what power Thy believing people of old used to pray, and what mighty wonders were done in answer to their prayers. And if this took place under the Old Covenant, in the time of preparation, how much more wilt Thou not now, in these days of fulfilment, give Thy people this sure sign of Thy presence in their midst. We have heard the promises given to Thine apostles of the power of prayer in Thy name, and have seen how gloriously they experienced their truth: we know for certain. they can become true to us too. We hear continually even in these days what glorious tokens of Thy power Thou dost still give to those who trust Thee fully. Lord! these all are men of like passions with ourselves; teach us to pray so too. The promises are for us, the powers and gifts of the heavenly world are for us. O teach us to pray so that we may receive abundantly. To us too Thou hast entrusted Thy work, on our prayer too the coming of Thy kingdom depends, in our prayer too Thou canst glorify Thy name; 'Lord, teach us to pray.' Yes, us, Lord; we offer ourselves as learners; we would indeed be taught of Thee. 'Lord, teach us to pray.'

'Lord, teach us to pray.' Yes, we feel the need now of being taught to pray. At first there is no work appears so simple; later on, none that is more difficult; and the confession is forced from us: We know not how to pray as we ought. It is true we have God's Word, with its clear and sure promises; but sin has so darkened our mind, that we know not always how to apply the Word. In spiritual things we do not always seek the most needful things, or fail in praying according to the law of the sanctuary. In temporal things we are still less able to avail ourselves of the wonderful liberty our Father has given us to ask what we need. And even when we know what to ask, how much there is still needed to make prayer acceptable. It must be to the glory of God, in full surrender to His will, in full assurance of faith, in the name of Jesus, and with a perseverance that, if need be, refuses to be denied. All this must be learned. It can only be learned in the school of much prayer, for practice makes perfect. Amid the painful consciousness of ignorance and unworthiness, in the struggle between believing and doubting, the heavenly art of effectual prayer is learned. Because, even when we do not remember it, there is One, the Beginner and Finisher of faith and prayer, who watches over our praying, and sees to it that in all who trust Him for it their education in the school of prayer shall be carried on to perfection. Let but the deep undertone of all our prayer be the teachable- that comes from a sense of ignorance, and from faith in Him as a perfect teacher, and we may be sure we shall be taught, we shall learn to pray in power. Yes, we may depend upon it, HE teaches to pray.

'Lord, teach us to pray.' None can teach like Jesus, none but Jesus; therefore we call on Him, `LORD, teach us to pray.' A pupil needs a teacher, who knows his work, who has the gift of teaching, who in patience and love will descend to the pupil's needs. Blessed be God! Jesus is a this and much more. He knows what prayer is. It is Jesus, praying Himself, who teaches to pray. He knows what prayer is. He learned it amid the trials and tears of His earthly life. In heaven it is still His beloved work: His life there is prayer. Nothing delights Him more than to find those whom He can take with Him into the Father's presence, whom He can clothe with power to pray down God's blessing on those around them, whom He can train to be His fellow-workers in the intercession by which the kingdom is to be revealed on earth. He knows how to teach.Now the urgency of felt need, then by the confidence with which joy inspires. Here by the teaching of the Word, there by the testimony of another believer who knows what it is to have prayer beard. By His Holy Spirit, He has access to our heart, and teaches us to pray by showing us the sin that hinders the prayer, or giving us the assurance than we please God. He teaches, by giving not only thoughts of what to ask or how to ask, but by breathing within us the very spirit of prayer, by living within us as the Great Intercessor. We may indeed and most joyfully say, `Who teacheth like Him?' Jesus never taught His disciples how to preach, only how to pray. He did not speak much of what was needed to preach well but much of praying well. To know how to speak to God is more than knowing how to speak to man. Not power with men; 'but power with God is,the first thing. Jesus loves to teach us how to pray:

What think you, my beloved fellow-disciples! would it not be just what we need, to ask the Master for a month to give us a course of special lessons on the art of prayer? As we meditate on the words He spake on earth, let us yield ourselves to His teaching in the fullest confidence that, with such a teacher, we shall make progress. Let us take time not only to meditate, but to pray, to tarry at the foot of the throne, and be trained to the work of intercession. Let us do so in the assurance that amidst our, stammerings and fears He is carrying on His work most beautifully. He will breathe His own life which is all prayer, into us. As he makes us partakers of His righteousness and His life, He will of His intercession too. As the members of His body,as a holy priesthood, we shall take part in His priestly work of pleading and prevailing with God for men. Yes, let us joyfully say, ignorant and feeble though we be, `Lord, teach us to pray:

Blessed Lord! who ever livest to pray, Thou canst teach me too to pray, me too to live ever to pray. In this Thou lovest to make me share Thy glory in heaven, that I should pray without ceasing, and ever stand as a priest in the presence of my God.

Lord Jesus! I ask Thee this day to enroll my name among those who confess that they know not how to pray as they ought, and specially ask Thee for a course of teaching in prayer.

Lord! teach me to tarry with Thee in the school, and give Thee time to train me. May a deep sense of my ignorance, of the wonderful privilege and power of prayer, of the need of the Holy Spirit as the Spirit of prayer, lead me to cast away my thoughts of what I think I know, and make me kneel before Thee in true teachableness and poverty of spirit.

And fill me, Lord, with the confidence that with such a teacher as Thou art I shall learn to pray. In the assurance that I have as my teacher, Jesus, who is ever praying to the Father, and by His prayer rules the destinies of His Church and the world, I will not be afraid. As much as I need to know of the mysteries of the prayer-world, Thou wilt unfold for me. And when I may not know, Thou wilt teach me to be strong in faith, giving glory to God.

Blessed Lord! Thou wilt not put to shame Thy scholar who trusts Thee, nor, by Thy grace, would he Thee either. Amen.

CHAPTER 2:
IN SPIRIT AND TRUTH OR
THE TRUE WORSHIPPERS

The hour cometh, and now is, when the true worshippers shall worship the Father in spirit and in truth: for such doth the Father seek to be worshippers. God is a Spirit: and they that worship Him must worship Him in spirit and truth.
-John 4:23-24

THESE WORDS OF JESUS TO THE WOMAN OF SAMARIA ARE His first recorded teaching on the subject of prayer. They give us some wonderful first glimpses into the word prayer. The Father seeks worshippers: our worship satisfies His loving heart and is a joy to Him. He seeks true worshippers, but finds many not as He would have them. True worship is that which is in spirit and truth. The Son has come to open the way for this worship in spirit and truth, and teach it to us. And so one of our first lessons in the school of prayer must be to understand what it is to pray in spirit and in truth and to know how we can attain to it.

To the woman of Samaria our Lord spoke of a threefold worship. There is first, the ignorant worship of the Samaritans:

'Ye worship that which ye know not.' The second, intelligent worship of the Jew, having the true knowledge of God: ' We worship that which we know; for salvation is of the Jews. And then the new, the spiritual worship which He Himself has come to introduce: `The hour is coming, and is now, when the true worshippers shall worship the Father in spirit and truth.' From the connection it is evident that the words `in spirit and truth do not mean, as is often thought, earnestly., from the heart, in sincerity. The Samaritans had the five books of Moses and some knowledge of God: there was doubtless more than one among them who honestly and earnestly sought God in prayer. The Jews had the true full revelation of God in His word, as thus given; there were among them godly men, who called upon God with their whole heart. And yet not `in spirit and truth,' in the full meaning of the words. Jesus says, `The hour is coming, and now is:' it is only in and through Him that the worship of God will be in spirit and truth.

Among Christians one still finds the three classes of worshippers. Some who in their ignorance hardly know what they ask: they pray earnestly, and yet receive but little.Others there are, who have more correct knowledge, who try to pray with all their mind and heart, and often pray more earnestly, and yet do not attain to the full blessedness of worship in spirit and truth. It is into this third class we must ask our Lord Jesus to take us; we must be taught of them how to worship in spirit and truth. This alone is spiritual worship; this makes us worshippers such as the Father seeks. In prayer everything will depend on our understanding well and practising the worship in spirit and truth.

'God is a Spirit, and they that worship Him, must worship Him in spirit and truth.' The first thought suggested here by the Master is that there must be harmony between God and His worshipers; -such as God is; must His worship be. This is according to a principle which prevails throughout the universe: we look for correspondence between an object and the organ to which it reveals or yields itself. The eye has an inner fitness for the light, the ear for sound. The man who would truly worship God, who would find and know and possess and enjoy God, must be in harmony with Him, must have the capacity for receiving Him. Because God is Spirit, we must worship in spirit. As God is, so His worshipper.

And what does this mean? The woman had asked our Lord whether Samaria or Jerusalem was the true place of worship. He answers that henceforth worship is no longer to be limited to a certain place: `Woman, believe Me, the hour cometh, when neither in this mountain, nor in Jerusalem shall ye worship the Father.' As God is Spirit, not bound by space or time but in His infinite perfection always and everywhere the same, so His worship would henceforth no longer be confined by place or form, but importance. How much our Christianity suffers from this, that it is confined to certain times and places. A man, who seeks to pray earnestly in the church or in the closet,spends the greater part of the week or the day in a spirit entirely at variance with that in which he prayed. His worship was the work of a fixed place or hour, not of his whole being. God is a Spirit: He is the Everlasting and Unchangeable One; what He is, He is always and in truth. Our worship must even so be in spirit and truth: His worship must be the spirit of our life; our life must be worship in spirit as God is Spirit.

God is a Spirit: and they that worship Him must worship Him in spirit and truth.' The second thought comes to us is that this worship in the spirit must come from God Himself. God is Spirit: He alone has Spirit to give: It was for this He sent His Son, to fit us for spiritual worship, by giving us the Holy Spirit. It is of His own work that Jesus speaks when He says twice, 'The hour cometh,' and then adds, 'and is now.' He came to baptize with the Holy Spirit; the Spirit could not stream forth until He was glorified (John 1.33, 7.37, 38, 16.7). It was when He had made an end of sin, and entering into the Holiest of all with His blood, had there on our behalf received the Holy Spirit (Acts 2.33), that He could send Him down to us as the Spirit of the Father. It was when Christ redeemed us, and we in Him had received the position of children, that the Father sent forth the Spirit of His Son into our hearts to cry, 'Abba, Father.' The worship in spirit is the worship of the Father in the Spirit of Christ, the Spirit of Sonship.

This is the reason why Jesus here uses the name Father. We never find one of the Old Testament saints personally appropriate the name of child or call God Father. The worship of the Father is only possible to those to whom the Spirit of the Son has been given. The worship in spirit is only possible to those to whom Son has revealed the Father, and who have received the spirit of Sonship. It is only Christ who opens the way and, teaches the worship in spirit.

And in truth. That does not only mean, in sincerity. Nor does

32

it only signify, in accordance with the truth of God's Word. The expression is one of deep and Divine meaning. Jesus is `the only-begotten of the Father, full of grace and truth: `The law was given by Moses, grace and truth came by Jesus Christ: Jesus says, `I am the truth and the life: In the Old Testament all was shadow and promise;Jesus brought and gives the reality, the substance, of things hoped for. In Him the blessings and powers of the eternal life are our actual possession and experience. Jesus is full of grace and truth; the Holy Spirit is the Spirit of truth;through Him the grace that is in Jesus is ours in deed and truth, a positive communication out of the Divine life. And so worship in spirit is worship in truth; actual living fellowship with God, a real correspondence and harmony-between the Father, who is a Spirit, and the child praying in the spirit.

What Jesus said to the woman of Samaria, she could not at once understand. Pentecost was needed to reveal its full meaning. We are hardly prepared at our first entrance into the school of prayer to grasp such teaching. We shall understand it better later on. Let us only begin and take the lesson as He gives it. We are carnal and cannot bring God the worship He seeks. But Jesus came to give the Spirit: He has given Him to us. Let the disposition in which we set ourselves to pray be what Christ's words have taught us. Let there be the deep confession of our inability to bring God the worship that is pleasing to Him; the childlike teachableness that waits on Him to instruct us; the simple faith that yields itself to the breathing of the Spirit. Above all, let us hold fast the blessed truth-we shall find that the Lord has more to say to us about it-that the knowledge of the Fatherhood of God, the revelation of His infinite Fatherliness in our hearts, the faith in the infinite love that gives us His Son and His Spirit to make us children, is indeed the secret of prayer in spirit and truth. This is the new and living way Christ opened up for us. To have Christ the Son, and the Spirit of the Son, dwelling within us, and revealing the Father, this makes us true, spiritual worshippers.

Blessed Lord! I adore the love with which Thou didst teach a woman, who had refused Thee a cup of water, what the worship of God must be. I rejoice in the assurance that Thou wilt no less now instruct Thy disciple, who comes to Thee with a heart that longs to pray in spirit and in truth. O my Holy Master! do teach me this blessed secret.

Teach me that the worship in spirit and truth is not of man, but only comes from Thee; that it is not only a thing of times and seasons, but the outflowing of a life in Thee. Teach me to draw near to God in prayer under the deep impression of my ignorance and my having nothing in myself to offer Him, and at the same time of the provision Thou my Saviour, makest for the Spirit's breathing in my childlike stammerings. I do bless Thee that in Thee I am a child, and have a child's liberty of access; that in Thee I have the spirit of Sonship and of worship in truth. Teach me, above all, Blessed Son of the Father, how it is the revelation of the Father that gives confidence in prayer; and let the infinite Fatherliness of God's Heart be my joy and strength for a life of prayer and of worship. Amen.

CHAPTER 3:
PRAY TO THY FATHER, WHICH IS IN SECRET OR ALONE WITH GOD

But thou, when thou prayest, enter into thine inner chamber, and having shut thy door, pray to thy Father which is in secret, and thy Father which seeth in secret shall recompense thee. -MATTHEW 6.6.

After Jesus had called His first disciples, He gave them their first public teaching in the Sermon on the Mount. He there expounded to them the kingdom of God, its laws and its life. In that kingdom God is not only King, but Father; He not only gives all, but is Himself all. In the knowledge and fellowship of Him alone is its blessedness. Hence it came as a matter of course that the revelation of prayer and the prayer-life was a part of His teaching concerning the New Kingdom He came to set up. Moses gave neither command nor regulation with regard to prayer: even the prophets say little directly of the duty of prayer; it is Christ who teaches to pray.

And the first thing the Lord teaches His disciples is that they must have a secret place for prayer ; every one must have some solitary spot where he can be alone with his God. Every teacher must have a schoolroom. We have learned to know and accept Jesus as our only teacher in the school of prayer. He has already taught us at Samaria that worship is no longer confined to times and places; that worship, spiritual true worship, is a thing of the spirit and the life; the whole man must in his whole life be worshipping in spirit and truth. And yet He wants each one to choose for himself the fixed spot where He can daily meet him. That inner chamber, that solitary place, is Jesus' schoolroom. That spot may be anywhere; that spot may change from day to day if we have to change our abode; but that secret place there must be, with the quiet time in which the pupil places himself in the Master's presence, to be by Him prepared to worship the Father. There alone, but there most surely, Jesus comes to us to teach us to pray.

A teacher is always anxious that his schoolroom should be bright and attractive, filled with the light and air of heaven, a place where pupils long to come, and love to stay. In His first words on prayer in the Sermon on the Mount, Jesus seeks to set the inner chamber before us in its most attractive light. If we listen carefully, we soon notice what the chief thing He has to tell us is of our tarrying there. Three times He uses the name of Father: `Pray to thy Father;' 'Thy Father shall recompense thee;' `Your Father knoweth what things ye have need of.' The first thing in closet-prayer is: I must meet my Father. The light that shines in the closet must be: the light of the Father's countenance. The fresh air from heaven with which Jesus would have it filled, the atmosphere in which I am to breathe and pray, is: God's Father-love, God's infinite

Fatherliness. Thus each thought or petition we breathe out will be simple, hearty, childlike trust in the Father. This is how the Master teaches us to pray: He brings us into the Father's living presence. What we pray there must avail. Let us listen carefully to hear what the Lord has to say to us.

First 'Pray to thy Father which is in secret.' God is a God who hides Himself to the carnal eye. As long as in our worship of God, we are chiefly occupied with our own thoughts and , exercises; we shall not meet Him who is a Spirit, the unseen One. But to the man who withdraws himself from all that is of the world and man, and prepares to wait upon God alone, the Father will reveal Himself. As he forsakes and gives up and shuts out the world, and the life of the world, and surrenders himself to be led of Christ into the secret of God's presence, the light of the Father's love will rise upon him. The secrecy of the inner chamber and the closed door, the entire separation from all around us, is an image of, and so a help to that inner spiritual sanctuary, the secret of God's tabernacle, within the veil, where our spirit truly comes into contact with the invisible One. And so we are taught, at the very outset of our search after the secret of effectual prayer, to remember that it is in the inner chamber; where we are alone with the Father, that we shall learn to pray aright. The Father is in secret: in these words Jesus teaches us where He is waiting for us, where He is always to be found. Christians often complain that private prayer is not what it should be. They feel weak and sinful, the heart is cold and dark; it is as if they have so little to pray, and in that little no faith or joy. They are discouraged and kept from prayer by the thought that they cannot come to the Father as they ought or as they wish. Child of God! listen to your Teacher. He tells you that when you go to private prayer your first thought must be: The Father is in secret, the Father awaits me there. Just because your heart is cold and prayerless, get into the presence of the loving Father. As a father pitieth his children so the Lord pitieth you. Do not be thinking of how little you have to bring God, but of how much He wants to give you. Just place yourself before, and look up into, His face; think of His love, His wonderful, tender, pitying love. Just tell Him how sinful and cold and dark all is: it is the Father's loving heart that will give light and warmth to yours. O do what Jesus says: Just shut the door, and pray to thy Father which is in secret. Is it not wonderful? to be able to go alone with God the infinite God, and then to look up and say: My Father!

`And thy Father, which seeth in secret, will recompense thee.' Here Jesus assures us that secret prayer cannot be fruitless: its blessing will show itself in our life. We have but in secret, alone with God, to entrust our life before men to Him; He will reward us openly; He will see to it that the answer to prayer be made manifest in His blessing upon us. Our Lord would thus teach us that as infinite Fatherliness and Faithfulness is that with which God meets us in secret, so on our part there should be the childlike simplicity of faith, the confidence that our prayer does bring down a blessing. He that cometh to God must believe that He is a rewarder of them that seek Him.' Not on the strong or the fervent feeling with which I pray does the blessing of the closet depend, but upon the love and the power of the Father to whom I there entrust my needs. And therefore the Master has but one desire: Remember your Father is, and sees and hears in secret; go there and stay there, and go again from there in the confidence: He will recompense. Trust Him for it; depend upon Him: prayer to the Father cannot be vain; He will reward you openly.

Still further to confirm this faith in the Father-love of God, Christ speaks a third word: 'Your Father knoweth what things ye have need of before ye ask Him.' At first sight it might appear as if this thought made prayer less needful: God knows far better than we what we need. But as we get a deeper insight into what prayer really is, this truth will help much to strengthen our faith. It will teach us that we do not need, as the heathen, with the multitude and urgency of our words, to compel an unwilling God to listen to us. It will lead to a holy thoughtfulness and silence in prayer as it suggests the question: Does my Father really know that I need this? It will, when once we have been led by the Spirit to the certainty that our request is indeed something that, according to the Word, we do need for God's glory, give us wonderful confidence to say, My Father knows I need it and must have it. And if there be any delay in the answer, it will teach us in quiet perseverance to hold on: Father thou knowest I need it. O the blessed liberty and simplicity of a child that Christ our Teacher would fain cultivate in us as we draw near to God: let us look up to the Father until His Spirit works it in us. Let us sometimes in our prayers, when we are in danger of being so occupied with our fervent, urgent petitions, as to forget that the Father knows and hears, let us hold still and just quietly say: My Father sees, my Father hears, my Father knows; it will help our faith to take the answer, and to say: We know that we have the petitions we have asked of Him.

And now, all ye who have anew entered the school of Christ to be taught to pray, take these lessons, practise them, and trust Him to perfect you in them. Dwell much in the inner chamber, with the door shut-shut in from men, shut up with God; it is there the Father waits you, it is there Jesus will teach you to pray. To be alone in secret with THE FATHER: this be your highest joy. To be assured that THE FATHER will openly reward the secret prayer, so that it cannot remain unblessed: this be your strength day by day. And to know that the Father knows that you need what you ask: this be your liberty to bring every need, in the assurance that your God will supply it according to His riches in glory in Christ Jesus.

Blessed Saviour! with my whole heart I do bless Thee for the appointment of the inner chamber, as the school where Thou meetest each of Thy pupils alone, and revealest to him the Father. O my Lord! strengthen my faith so in the Father's tender love and kindness, that as often as I feel sinful or troubled, the first instinctive thought may be to go where I know the Father wafts me, and where prayer never can go unblessed. Let the thought that He knows my need before I ask, bring me, in great restfulness Of faith, to trust that He will give what His child requires. O let the place of secret prayer become to me the most beloved spot of earth.

And, Lord! hear me as I pray that Thou wouldest everywhere bless the closets of Thy believing people. Let Thy wonderful revelation of a Father's tenderness free all young Christians from every thought of secret prayer as a duty or a burden, and lead them to regard it as the highest privilege of their life, a joy and a blessing. Bring back all who are discouraged, because they cannot find ought to bring Thee in prayer. O give them to understand that they have only to come with their emptiness to Him who has all to give, and delights to do it. Not, what they have to bring the Father, but what the Father waits to give them, be their one thought.

And bless especially the inner chamber of all Thy servants who are working for Thee, as the place where God's truth and God's grace are revealed to them, where they are daily anointed with fresh oil, where their strength is renewed, and the blessings are received in faith, with which they are to bless their fellow-men. Lord; draw us all in the closet nearer to Thyself and the Father. Amen.

CHAPTER 4:
AFTER THIS MANNER PRAY
OR THE MODEL PRAYER

After this manner therefore pray ye: Our Father, which art in heaven. -MATTHEW 6.9.

EVERY TEACHER KNOWS THE POWER OF EXAMPLE. HE NOT only tells the child what to do and how to do it, but shows him how it really can be done. In condescension to our weakness, our Heavenly Teacher has given us the very words we are to take with us as we draw near to our Father. We have in them a form of prayer in which there breathe the freshness and fulness of the Eternal Life. So simple that the child can lisp it, so divinely rich that it comprehends all that God can give. A form of prayer that becomes the model and inspiration for all other prayer, and yet always draws us back to itself as the deepest utterance of our souls before our God.

`Our Father which art in heaven!' To appreciate this word of adoration aright, I must remember that none of the saints had in Scripture ever ventured to address God as their Father. The invocation places us at once in the centre of the wonderful revelation the Son came to make of His Father as our Father too. It comprehends the mystery of redemption-Christ delivering us from the curse that we might become the children of God. The mystery of regeneration-the Spirit in the new birth giving us the new life. And the mystery of faith-ere yet the redemption is accomplished or understood the word is given on the lips of the disciples to prepare them for the blessed experience still to come. The words are the key to the whole prayer, to all prayer. It takes time, it takes life to study them; it will take eternity to understand them fully. The knowledge of God's Father-love is the first and simplest, but also the last and highest lesson in the school of prayer. It is in the personal relation to the living God, and the personal conscious fellowship of love with Himself, that prayer begins. It is in the knowledge of God's Fatherliness, revealed by the Holy Spirit, that the power of prayer will be found to root and grow. In the infinite tenderness and pity and patience of the infinite Father, in His loving readiness to hear and to help, the life of prayer has its joy. O let us take time, until the Spirit has made these words to us spirit and truth, filling heart and life: Our Father which art in heaven.' Then we are indeed within the veil, in the secret place of power where prayer always prevails.

`Hallowed be Thy name.' There is something here that strikes us at once. While we ordinarily first bring our own needs to God in prayer, and then think of what belongs to God and His interests, the Master reverses the order. First, Thy name, Thy kingdom, Thy will; then, give us, forgive us, lead us, deliver us. The lesson is of more importance than we think. In true worship the Father must be first,must be all. The sooner I

44

learn to forget myself in the desire that HE may be glorified, the richer will the blessing be that prayer will bring to myself. No one ever loses by what he sacrifices for the Father.

This must influence all our prayer. There are two sorts of prayer: personal and intercessory. The latter ordinarily occupies the lesser part of our time and energy. This may not be. Christ has opened the school of prayer specially to train intercessors for the great work of bringing down, by their faith and prayer, the blessings of His work and love on the world around. There can be no deep growth in prayer unless this be made our aim. The little child may ask of the father only what it needs for itself; and yet it soon learns to say, give some for sister too. But the grownup son, who only lives for the father's interest and takes charge of the father's business, asks more largely, and gets all that is asked. And Jesus would train us to the blessed life of consecration and service, in which our interests are all subordinate to the Name, and the Kingdom, and the Will of the Father. O let us live for this and let, on each act of adoration, Our Father! there follow in the same breath, Thy Name, Thy Kingdom, Thy Will;-for this we look up and long.

Hallowed be Thy name.' What name? This new name of Father. The word Holy is the central word of the Old Testament; the name Father of the New. In this name of Love all the holiness and glory of God are now to be revealed. And how is the name to be hallowed? By God Himself: `I will hallow My great name which ye have profaned.' Our prayer must be that in ourselves in all God's children, in presence of the world, God Himself would reveal the holiness, the Divine power, the hidden glory of the name of Father. The Spirit of the Father is the Holy Spirit: it is only when we yield ourselves to be led of Him, that the name will be hallowed in our prayers and our lives. Let us learn the prayer: 'Our Father, hallowed be Thy name.'

'Thy kingdom come.' The Father is a King and has a kingdom. The son and heir of a king has no higher ambition than the glory of his father's kingdom. In time of war or danger this becomes his passion; he can think of nothing else. The children of the Father are here in the enemy's territory, where the kingdom, which is in heaven, is not yet fully manifested. What more natural than that, when they learn to hallow the Father-name, they should long and cry with deep enthusiasm: 'Thy kingdom come. The coming of the kingdom is the one great event on which the revelation of the Father's glory, the blessedness of His children, the salvation of the world depends. On our prayers too the coming of the kingdom waits. Shall we not join in the deep longing cry of the redeemed: 'Thy kingdom come'? Let us learn it in the school of Jesus.

'Thy will be done, as in heaven, so on earth.' This petition is too frequently applied alone to the suffering of the will of God. In heaven God's will is done, and the Master teaches the child to ask that the will may be done on earth just as in heaven: in the spirit of adoring submission and ready obedience. Because the will of God is the glory of heaven the doing of it is the blessedness of heaven. As the will is done,- the kingdom of heaven comes into the heart. And whereever faith has accepted the Father's love, obedience accepts the

46

Father's will. The surrender to, and the prayer for a life of heaven-like obedience, is the spirit of childlike prayer.

`Give us this day our daily bread! When first the child has yielded himself to the Father in the care for His Name, His Kingdom, and His Will, he has full liberty to ask for his daily bread. A master cares for the food of his servant, a general of his soldiers, a father of his child. And will not the Father in heaven care for the child who has in prayer given himself up to His interests? We may indeed in full confidence say: Father, I live for Thy honour and Thy work; I know Thou carest for me. Consecration to God and His will gives wonderful liberty in prayer for temporal things: the whole earthly life is given to the Father's loving care.

`And forgive us our debts, as we also have forgiven our debtors. As bread is the first need of the body, so forgiveness for the soul, And the provision for the one is as sure as for the other. We are children, but sinners too; our right of access to the Father's presence we owe to the precious blood and the forgiveness it has won for us. Let us beware of the prayer for forgiveness becoming a formality: only what is really confessed is really forgiven. Let us in faith accept the forgiveness as promised: as a spiritual reality, an actual transaction between God and us, it is the entrance into all the Father's love and all the privileges of children. Such forgiveness, as a living experience, is impossible without a forgiving spirit to others: as forgiven expresses the heavenward, so forgiving the earthward, relation of God's child. In each prayer to the Father I must be able to say that I know of no one whom I do not heartily love.

`And lead us not into temptation, but deliver us from the evil one.' Our daily bread, the pardon of our sins, and then our being kept from all sin and the power of the evil one, in these three petitions all our personal need is comprehended. The prayer for bread and pardon must be accompanied by the surrender to live in all things in holy obedience to the Father's will, and the believing prayer in everything to be kept by the power of the indwelling Spirit from the power of the evil one.

Children of God! it is thus Jesus would have us to pray to the Father in heaven. O let His Name, and Kingdom, and Will, have the first place in our love; His providing, and pardoning, and keeping love will be our sure portion, So the prayer will lead us up to the true childlife: the Father all to the child, the Father all for the child. We shall understand how Father and child, the Thine and the our, are all one, and how the heart that begins its prayer with the God-devoted Thine, will have the power in faith to speak out the Our too. Such prayer will, indeed, be the fellowship and interchange of love, always bringing us back in trust and worship to Him who is not only the Beginning but the End:' For Thine is the Kingdom and the Power, and the Glory, for ever Amen.' Son of the Father, teach us to pray, 'Our Father'.

O Thou who art the only-begotten Son, teach us, we beseech Thee, to pray, 'Our FATHER.' We thank Thee, Lord, for these Living Blessed Words which Thou hast given us. We thank Thee for the millions who in them have learnt to know and worship the Father, and for what they have been to us. Lord! it is as if we needed days and weeks in Thy school with each separate petition; so deep and full are they. But we look to

48

Thee to lead us deeper into their meaning: do it, we pray Thee, for Thy Name's sake; Thy name is Son of the Father.

Lord! Thou didst once say: `No man knoweth the Father save the Son, and he to whom the Son willeth to reveal Him.' And again: `I made known unto them Thy name, and will make it known, that the love wherewith Thou hast loved Me may be in them.' Lord Jesus! reveal to us the Father. Let His name, His infinite Father-love, the love with which He loved Thee, according to Thy prayer, BE IN us. Then shall we say aright, `OUR Father!'

Then shall we apprehend Thy teaching and the first spontaneous breathing of our heart will be: `Our Father, Thy Name, Thy Kingdom, Thy Will.' And we shall bring our needs and our sins and our temptations to Him in the confidence that the love of such a Father cares for all.

Blessed Lord! we are Thy scholars, we trust Thee; do teach us to pray, 'Our Father.' Amen.

CHAPTER 5:
ASK AND IT SHALL BE GIVEN YOU OR THE CERTAINTY OF THE ANSWER TO PRAYER

'Ask, and it shall be given you; seek, and ye shall find; knock and it shall be opened unto you :for every one that asketh receiveth and he that seeketh findeth ; and to him that knocketh it shall opened.' -Matthew 7:7-8

Ye ask, and receive not, because ye ask amiss.' -James 4:3

OUR Lord returns here in the Sermon the Mount a second time to speak of prayer. The first time He had spoken of the Father who is to be found in secret, and rewards openly, and has given us the pattern prayer (Matt. 6:5). Here He wants to teach us what in all Scripture is considered the chief thing in prayer: the assurance that prayer will be heard and answered. Observe how He uses words which mean almost the same thing, and each time repeats the promise distinctly: ` Ye shall receive, ye shall find, it shall be opened unto you;' and then gives us ground for such assurance the law of the kingdom: ` He that asketh receiveth ; he that seeketh, findeth to him that knocketh, it shall he opened. We cannot but feel how in this

51

sixfold repetition He wants to impress deep on our minds this one truth, that we may and must most confidently expect an answer to our prayer. Next to the revelation of the Father's love, there is, in the whole course of the school of prayer, not a more important lesson than this: Every one that asketh, receiveth.

In the three words the Lord uses, ask, seek, knock, a difference in meaning has been sought. If such was indeed His purpose, then the first, ASK, refers to the gifts we pray for. But I may ask and receive the gift without the Giver. Seek is the word Scripture uses of God Himself; Christ assures me that I can find Himself. But it is not enough to find God in time of need, without coming to abiding fellowship: KNOCK speaks of admission to dwell with Him and in Him. Asking and receiving the gift would thus lead to seeking and finding the Giver, and this again to the knocking and opening of the door of the Father's home and love. One thing is sure : the Lord does want us to count most certainly on it that asking, seeking, knocking, cannot be in vain: receiving an answer, finding God, the opened heart and home of God, are the certain fruit of prayer.

That the Lord should have thought it needful in so many forms to repeat the truth, is a lesson of deep import. It proves that He knows our heart, how doubt and distrust toward God are natural to us, and how easily we are inclined to rest in prayer as a religious work without an answer. He knows too how even when we believe that God is the Hearer of prayer, believing prayer that lays hold of the promise, is something spiritual, too high and difficult for the halfhearted disciple.

He therefore at the very outset of His instruction to those who would learn to pray, seeks to lodge this truth deep into their hearts: prayer does avail much; ask and ye shall receive; every one that asketh, receiveth. This is the fixed eternal law of the kingdom: if you ask and receive not, it must be because there is something amiss or wanting in the prayer. Hold on; let the word and Spirit teach you to pray aright, but do not let go the confidence He seeks to waken: Every one that asketh, receiveth.

'Ask, and it shall be given you.' Christ has no mightier stimulus to persevering prayer in His school than this. As a child has to prove a sum to be correct, so the proof that we have prayed aright is, the answer. If we ask and receive not, it is because we have not learned to pray aright. Let every learner in the school of Christ therefore take the Master's word in all simplicity: Every one that asketh, receiveth. He had good reasons for speaking so unconditionally. Let us beware of weakening the Word with our human wisdom. When He tells us heavenly things, let us believe Him. His Word will explain itself to him who believes it fully. If questions and difficulties arise, let us not seek to have them settled before we accept the Word. No; let us entrust them all to Him: it is His to solve them: our work is first and fully to accept and hold fast His promise. Let in our inner chamber, in the inner chamber of our heart too, the Word be inscribed in letters of light, Every one that asketh, receiveth.

According to this teaching of the Master, prayer consists of two parts, has two sides, a human and a Divine. The human is the asking, the Divine is the giving. Or, to look at both from the human side, there is the asking and the receiving-the two halves that make up a whole. It is as if He would tell us that we are not to rest without an answer, because it is the will of God, the rule in the Father's family : every childlike believing petition is granted. If no answer comes, we are not to sit down in the cloth that calls itself resignation, and suppose that it is not God's will to give an answer. No; there must be something in the prayer that is not as God would have it, childlike and believing; we must seek for grace to pray so that the answer may come. It is far easier to the flesh to submit without the answer than to yield itself to be searched and purified by the Spirit, until it has learnt to pray the prayer of faith.

It is one of the terrible marks of the diseased state of Christian life in these days, that there are so many who rest content without the distinct experience of answer to prayer. They pray daily, they ask many things, and trust that some of them will be heard, but know little of direct definite answer to prayer as the rule of daily life. And it is this the Father wills ; He seeks daily intercourse with His children in listening to and granting their petitions.He wills that I should come to Him day by day with distinct requests; He wills day by day to do for me what I ask.It was in His answer to prayer that the saints of old learned to know God as the Living One, and were stirred to praise and love (Psalm 34, Psalm 66:19, Psalm 116:1) Our Teacher waits to imprint this upon our minds; prayer and its answer, the child asking and the father giving, belong to each other.

There may be cases in which the answer is a refusals, because the request is not according to God's Word, as when Moses asked to enter Canaan. But still there was an answer: God did not leave His servant in uncertainty as to His will. The gods of the heathen are dumb and cannot speak. Our Father lets His child know when He cannot give him what he asks, and he withdraws his petition, even as the Son did in Gethsemane. Both Moses the servant and Christ the Son knew that what they asked was not according to what 'the Lord had spoken: their prayer was the humble supplication whether it was not possible for the decision to be changed. God will teach those who are teach able and give Him time, by His Word and Spirit, whether their request be according to His will or not. Let us withdraw the request, if it be not according God's mind, or persevere till the answer come. Prayer is appointed to obtain the answer. It is in prayer and its answer that the interchange of love between .the Father and His child takes place.

How deep the estrangement of our heart from God must be, that we find it so difficult to grasp such promises, even while we accept the words and believe their truth, the faith of the heart, that fully has them and rejoices in them, comes so slowly. It is because our spiritual life is still so weak, and the capacity for taking God's thoughts is so feeble. But let us look to Jesus to teach us as none but He can teach. If we take His words in simplicity, and trust Him by his Spirit to make them within us life and power, they will so enter into our inner being, to the spiritual Divine reality of the truth they contain will indeed take possession of us, and we shall not rest content until every petition we offer is borne heavenward on Jesus' own words ` Ask, and it shall be given you.'

Beloved fellow-disciples in the school of Jesus, let us set

ourselves to learn this lesson well. Let us take these words just as they were spoken. Let us not suffer human reason to weaken their force. Let us take these words as Jesus gives them, and believe them. He will teach us in due time how to understand them fully: let us begin by implicitly believing them. Let us take time, often as we pray, to listen to His voice: Every one that asketh, receiveth. Let. us not make the feeble experiences of our unbelief the measure of what our faith may expect. Let us seek, not only just in our seasons of prayer, but at all times, to hold fast the joyful assurance: man's prayer on earth and God's answer in heaven are meant for each other. Let us trust Jesus to teach us so too pray,that the answer can come. He will do it, if we hold fast the word He gives today : ` Ask, and ye shall receive.'

LORD, TEACH UP TO PRAY!

0 Lord Jesus! teach me to understand and believe what Thou hast now promised me. It is not hid from Thee, 0 my Lord, with what reasonings my heart seeks to satisfy itself, when no answer comes. There is the thought that my prayer is not in harmony with the Father's secret counsel ; that there is perhaps something better Thou wouldest give me; or that prayer as fellowship with God is blessing enough without an answer And yet, my blessed Lord, I find in Thy teaching on prayer that Thou didst not speak of these things, but didst say so plainly, that prayer may and must expect an answer. Thou doth assure us that this is the fellowship of a child with the Father; the child asks and the Father gives.

Blessed Lord ! Thy words are faithful and true. It must be,

because I pray amiss, that my experience of answered prayer is not clearer. It must be, because I live too little in the Spirit, that my prayer is too little in the Spirit, and that the power for the prayer of faith is wanting.

Lord ! teach me to pray. Lord Jesus! I trust Thee for it; teach me to pray in faith. Lord teach me this lesson of to-day! Every one that asketh, receiveth. Amen.

CHAPTER 6:
HOW MUCH MORE? ' OR THE INFINITE FATHERLINESS OF GOD

'Or what man is there of you, who, if his son ask him for a loaf, will give him a stone; or if he shall ask for a fish, will give him a serpent! If ye then, being evil, know how to give good gifts unto your children, how much more shall your Father which is in Heaven give good things to them that ask Him!' -Matthew 7:9-11

In these words our Lord proceeds further to confirm what He said of the certainty of an answer to prayer. To remove all doubt, and show us on what sure ground His promise rests, He appeals to what every one has seen and experienced here on earth. We are all children, and know what we expected of our fathers. We are fathers, or continually see them ; and everywhere we look upon it as the most natural thing there can be, for a father to hear his child. And the Lord asks us to look up from earthly parents, of whom the best are but evil, and to calculate How much more the heavenly Father will give good gifts to them that ask Him. Jesus would lead us up to see, that as much greater as God is than sinful man, so much greater our assurance ought to be that He will more surely than any earthly father grant our childlike petitions. As much greater as God is than man, so much surer is that prayer will be heard with the Father in heaven than with a father on earth.

As simple and intelligible as this parable is, so deep and spiritual is the teaching it contains. The Lord would remind us that the prayer of a child owes its influence entirely to the relation in which he stands to the parent. The prayer can exert that influence only when the child is really living in that relationship, in the home, in the love, in the service of the Father. The power of the promise, 'Ask, and it shall be given you,' lies in the loving relationship between us as children and the Father in heaven; when we live and walk in that relationship, the prayer of faith and its answer will be the natural result. And so the lesson we have today in the school of prayer is this : Live as a child of God,then you will be able to pray as a child, and as a child you will most assuredly be heard.

And what is the true child-life ? The answer can be found in any home. The child that by preference forsakes the father's house, that finds no pleasure in the presence and love and obedience of the father, and still thinks to ask and obtain what he will, will surely be disappointed. On the contrary, he to whom the intercourse and will and honour and love of the father are the joy of his life, will find that it is the father's joy to grant his requests. Scripture says, ' As many as are led by the Spirit of God, they are the children of God:' the childlike privilege of asking all is inseparable from the childlike life under the leading of the Spirit. He that gives himself to be led by the Spirit in his life, will be led by Him in his prayers too. And he will find that Fatherlike giving is the Divine response to childlike living.

To see what this childlike living is, in which childlike asking and believing have their ground, we have only to notice what our Lord teaches in the Sermon on the Mount of the Father and His children. In it the prayer-promises are imbedded in the life-precepts; the two are inseparable. They form one whole; and He alone can count on the fulfilment of the promise, who accepts too all that the Lord has connected with it. It is as if in speaking the word, `.Ask, and ye shall receive,' He says: I give these promises to those whom in the beatitudes I have pictured in their childlike poverty and purity, and of whom I have said, 'They shall be called the children of God' (Matt. 5: 3-9): to children, who 'let your light shine before men, so that they may glorify your Father in heaven:' to those who walk in love, 'that ye may be children of your Father which is in heaven,' and who seek to be perfect ` even as your Father in heaven is perfect' (v. 45) : to those whose fasting and praying and almsgiving (6: 1-18) is not before men, but ' before your Father which seeth in secret;' who forgive even as your Father forgiveth you' (6:15);who trust the heavenly Father in righteousness (6:26-32); who not only say, Lord,

Lord, but do the will of my Father which is in heaven (7:21). Such are the children of the Father, and such is the life in the Father's love and service; in such a child-life, answered prayers are certain and abundant.

But will not such teaching discourage the feeble one? If we are first to answer to this portrait of a child, must not many give up all hope of answers to prayer? The difficulty is removed if we think again of the blessed name of father and child. A child is weak; there is a great difference among children in age and gift. The Lord does not demand of us a perfect fulfilment of the law; no, but ony the childlike and whole-hearted surrender to live as a child with Him in obedience and truth. Nothing more. But also,nothing less. The Father must have the whole heart. When this is given, and He sees the child with honest purpose and steady will seeking in everything to be and live as a child, then our prayer will count with Him as the prayer of a child. Let any one simply and honestly begin to study the sermon on the Mount and take it as his guide in life, and he will find, notwithstanding weakness and failure, an ever-growing liberty to claim the fulfilment of its promises in regard to prayer. In the names of father and child he has the pledge that his petitions will be granted.

This is the one chief thought on which Jesus dwells here, and which He would have all His scholars take in. He would have us see that the secret of effectual prayer is: to have the heart filled with the Father-love of God. It is not enough for us to know that God is a Father: He would have us take time to come under the full impression of what that name implies. We must take the best earthly father we know; we must think of the tenderness and love with which he regards the request of his child, the love and joy with which he grants every reasonable desire; we must then, as we think in adoring worship of the infinite Love and Fatherliness of God, consider with how much more tenderness and joy He sees us come to Him, and gives us what we ask aright. And then, when we see how much this Divine arithmetic is beyond our comprehension, and feel how impossible it is for us to apprehend God's readiness to hear us, then He would have us come and open our heart for the Holy Spirit to shed abroad God's Father-love there. Let us do this not only when we want to pray, but let us yield heart and life to dwell in that love. The child who only wants to know the love of the father when he has something to ask, will be disappointed. But he who lets God be Father always and in everything, who would fain live his whole life in the Father's presence and love, who allows God in all the greatness of His love to be a Father to him, oh! he will experience most gloriously that a life in God's infinite Fatherliness and continual answers to prayer are inseparable.

Beloved fellow-disciple! we begin to see what the reason is that we know so little of daily answers to prayer, and what the chief lesson is which the Lord has for us in His school. It is all in the name of Father. We thought of new and deeper insight into some of the mysteries of the prayerworld as what we should get in Christ's school; He tells us the first is the highest lesson; we must learn to say well, ' Abba, Father!' 'Our Father which art in heaven.' He that can say this, has the key to all prayer. In all the compassion with which a father listens to his weak or sickly child, in all the joy with which he hears his stammering child, in all the gentle patience with which he bears with a thoughtless child, we must, as in so many mirrors, study the heart of our Father, until every prayer be borne upward on the faith of this Divine word: 'How much more shall your heavenly Father give good gifts to them that ask Him.'

' LORD, TEACH US TO PRAY.'

Blessed Lord! Thou knowest that this, though it be one of the first and simplest and most glorious lessons in Thy school, is to our hearts one of the hardest to learn: we know so little of the love of the Father. Lord! teach us so to live with the Father that His love may be to us nearer, clearer, dearer, than the love of any earthly father. And let the assurance of His hearing our prayer be as much greater than the confidence in an earthly parent, as the heavens are higher than earth, as God is infinitely greater than man. Lord! show us that it is only our unchildlike distance from the Father that hinders the answer to prayer, and lead us on to the true life of God's children. Lord Jesus ! it is fatherlike love that wakens childlike trust. O reveal to us the Father, and His tender, pitying love, that we may become childlike, and experience how in the child-life lies the power of prayer.

Blessed Son of God! the Father loveth Thee and hath given Thee all things. And Thou lovest the Father, and hast done all things He commanded Thee, and therefore hast the power to ask all things. Lord! give us Thine own Spirit, the Spirit of the Son. Make us childlike, as Thou wert on earth. And let every prayer be breathed in the faith that as the heaven is higher than the earth, so God's Father-love, and His readiness to give us what we ask, surpasses all we can think or conceive. Amen,

CHAPTER 7:
HOW MUCH MORE THE HOLY SPIRIT OR THE ALL COMPREHENSIVE GIFT

If ye then, being evil, know how to give good gifts unto your children, how much more shall the heavenly Father give the Holy Spirit to them that ask Him! -Luke 11:13

In the Sermon on the Mount, the Lord had already given utterance to His wonderful How much more? Here in Luke, where He repeats the question, there is a difference. Instead of speaking, as then, of giving good gifts, He says, 'How much more shall the heavenly Father give THE HOLY SPIRIT?' He thus teaches us that the chief and the best of these gifts is the Holy Spirit, or rather, that in this gift all others are comprised. The Holy Spirit is the first of the Father's gifts, and the one He delights most to bestow. The Holy Spirit is therefore the gift we ought first and chiefly to seek.

The unspeakable worth of this gift we can easily understand. Jesus spoke of the Spirit as 'the promise of the Father;' the one promise in which God's Fatherhood revealed itself. The best gift a good and wise father can bestow on a child on earth is his own spirit. This is the great object of a father in education---. to reproduce in his child his own disposition and character. If the child is to know and understand his father; if, as he grows up, he is to enter into all his will and plans; if he is to have his highest joy in the father, and the father in him,--he must be of one mind and spirit with him. And so it is impossible to conceive of God bestowing any higher gift on His child than this, His own Spirit. God is what He is through His Spirit; the Spirit is the very life of God. Just think what it means--God giving His own Spirit to His child on earth.

Or was not this the glory of Jesus as a Son upon earth, that the Spirit of the Father was in Him ? At His baptism in Jordan the two things were united,---.the voice, proclaiming Him the Beloved Son, and the Spirit, descending upon Him, And so the apostle says of us, ` Because ye are sons, God sent forth the Spirit of His Son into your hearts, crying, Abba, Father.' A king seeks in the whole education of his son to call forth in him a kingly spirit. Our Father in heaven desires to educate us as His children for the holy, heavenly life in which He dwells, and for this gives us, from the depths of His heart, His own Spirit. It was this which was the whole aim of Jesus when, after having made atonement with His own blood, He entered for us into God's presence. that He might obtain for us, and send down to dwell in us, the Holy Spirit. As the Spirit of the Father, and the Son, the whole life and love of the Father and the Son are in Him ; and coming down into us, He lifts us up into their fellowship. As Spirit of the Father, He sheds abroad the Father's love, with which He loved the Son, in our hearts, and teaches us to live in it. As Spirit of the Son, He breaths in us the childlike liberty, and devotion, and obedience in which the Son lived upon earth. The Father can bestow no higher or more wonderful gift than this: His own Holy Spirit, the Spirit of sonship.

This truth naturally suggests the thought that this first and chief gift of God must be the first and chief object of all prayer. For every need of the spiritual life this is the one thing needful:the Holy Spirit. All the fulness is in Jesus; the fulness of grace and truth, out of which we receive, grace for grace. The Holy Spirit is the appointed conveyancer, whose special work it is to make Jesus and all there is in Him for us ours in personal appropriation, in blessed experience. He is the Spirit of life in Christ Jesus; as wonderful as the life is, so wonderful is the provision by which such an agent is provided to communicate it to us. If we but yield ourselves entirely to the disposal of the Spirit,and let Him have His way with us, He will manifest the life of Christ within us. He will do this with a Divine power, maintaining the life of Christ in us in uninterrupted continuity. Surely, if there is one prayer that should draw us to the Father's throne and keep us there, it is this: for the Holy Spirit, whom we as children have received, to stream into us and out from us in greater fulness.

In the variety of the gifts which the Spirit has to dispense, He meets the believer's every need: Just think of the names He bears. The Spirit of grace, to reveal and impart all of grace there is in Jesus. The Spirit of faith, teaching us to begin,and go on and increase in ever believing. The Spirit of adoption and assurance, who witnesses that we are God's children, and inspires the confiding and confident Abba Father! The Spirit of truth, to lead into all truth, to make each word of God ours in deed and in truth. The Spirit of prayer, through whom we speak with the Father;prayer that must be heard. The Spirit of judgment and burning, to search the heart, and convince of sin. The Spirit of holiness, manifesting and communicating the Father's holy presence within us. The Spirit of power, through whom we are strong to testify boldly and work effectually in the Father's service. The Spirit of glory, the pledge of our inheritance, the preparation and the foretaste of the glory to come. Surely the child of God needs but one thing to be able really to live as a child: it is, to be filled with this Spirit.

And now, the lesson Jesus teaches us today in His school is this: That the Father is just longing to give Him to us if we will but ask in the childlike dependence on what He says: ' If ye know to give good gifts unto your children, HOW MUCH MORE shall your heavenly Father gave the holy Spirit to them that ask Him.' In the words of God's promise, 'I will pour out my Spirit abundantly; 'and of His command, ' Be ye filled with the Spirit,' we have the measure of what God is ready to give, and what we may obtain. As God's children, we have already received the Spirit. But we still need to ask and pray for His special gifts and operations as we require them. And not only this, but for Himself to take complete and entire possession; for His unceasing momentary guidance. Just as the branch, already filled with the sap of the vine, is ever crying for the continued and increasing flow of that sap, that it may bring its fruit to perfection, so the believer, rejoicing in the possession of the Spirit, ever thirsts and cries for more. And what the great Teacher would have us learn is, that nothing less than God's promise and God's command may be the measure of our expectation and our prayer; we must be filled abundantly. He would have us ask this in the assurance that the wonderful How much more of God's Father-love is the pledge that, when we ask, we do most certainly receive.

Let us now believe this. As we pray to be filled with the Spirit, let us not seek for the answer in our feelings. All spiritual blessings must be received, that is, accepted or taken in faith.' Let me believe, the Father gives the Holy Spirit to His praying child. Even now, while I pray, I must say in faith:I have what I ask, the fulness of the Spirit is mine. Let us continue stedfast in this faith. On the strength of God's Word we know that we have what we ask. Let us, with thanksgiving that we have been heard, with thanksgiving for what we have received and taken and now hold as ours, continue stedfast in believing prayer that the blessing, which has already been given us, and which we hold in faith, may break through and fill our whole being. It is in such believing thanksgiving and prayer, that our soul opens up for the Spirit to take entire and undisturbed possession. It is such prayer that not only asks and hopes, but takes and holds, that inherits the full blessing. In all our prayer let us remember the lesson the Saviour would teach us this day; that, if there is one thing on earth we can be sure of, it is this, that the Father desires to have us filled' with His Spirit, that He delights to give us His Spirit.

And when once we have learned thus to believe for ourselves, and each day to take out of the treasure, we hold in heaven, what liberty and power to pray for the outpouring of the Spirit on the Church of God, on all flesh, on individuals, or on

69

special efforts! He that has once learned to know the Father in prayer for himself, learns to pray most confidently for others too. The Father gives the Holy Spirit to them that asks Him, not least, but most, when they ask for others.

LORD, TEACH US TO PRAY!

Father in heaven ! Thou didst send Thy Son to reveal Thyself to us, Thy Father-love, and all that that love has for us. And He has taught us, that the gift above all gifts which Thou wouldest bestow in answer to prayer is, the Holy Spirit.

O my Father! I come to Thee with this prayer; there is nothing I would--may I not say, I do-- desire so much as to be filled with the Spirit, the Holy Spirit. The blessings He brings are so unspeakable and just what I need. He sheds abroad Thy love in the heart, and fills it with Thyself. I long for this. He breathes the mind and life of Christ in me, so that I live as He did, in and for the Father's love. I long for this. He endues with power from on high for all my walk and work. I long for this, O Father ! I beseech Thee,give me this day the fulness of Thy Spirit.

Father! I ask this, resting on the words of my Lord : ` How much more the Holy Spirit!' I do believe that Thou hearest my prayer; I receive now what I ask; Father! I claim and I take it: the fulness of Thy Spirit as mine. I receive the gift this day again as a faith gift; in faith I reckon my Father works through the Spirit all He has promised. The Father delights to breathe His Spirit into His waiting child as He tarries in fellowship with Himself. Amen

CHAPTER 8:
BECAUSE OF HIS IMPORTUNITY OR THE BOLDNESS OF GOD'S FRIENDS

And He said unto them, Which of you shall have a friend, and shall go to him at midnight, and say to him, Friend, lend me three loaves; for a friend of mine is come to me from a journey, and I have nothing to set before him; and he from within shall answer and say, Trouble me not: the door is now shut, and my children are with me in bed; I cannot rise and give thee. 1 say unto you though he will not rise and give him because he is his friend, yet because of his importunity he will rise and give him as many as he needeth: -LUKE 11.5-8.

THE FIRST TEACHING TO HIS DISCIPLES WAS GIVEN BY OUR Lord in the Sermon on the Mount. It was nearly a year later that the disciples asked Jesus to teach them to pray. In answer He gave them a second time the Lord's prayer, so teaching them what to pray. He then speaks of how they ought to pray, and repeats what he formerly said of God's Fatherliness and the certainty of an answer. But in between He adds the beautiful parable of the friend at midnight, to teach them the twofold lesson, that God does not only want us to pray for ourselves, but for the perishing around us, and that in such intercession great boldness of entreaty is often needful, and always lawful yea, pleasing to God.

The parable is a perfect storehouse of instruction in regard to true intercession. There is, first, the love which seeks to help the needy around us: `my friend is come to me.' Then the need which urges to the cry: I have nothing to set before him.' Then follows the confidence that help is to be had: `which of you shall ask a friend and say, Friend, lend me three loaves.' Then comes the unexpected refusal; `I cannot rise and give thee.' Then again the Perseverance that takes no refusal: `because of his importunity. And lastly, the reward of such prayer: `he will give him as many as he needeth.' A wonderful setting forth of the way of prayer and faith in which the blessing of God has so often been sought and found.

Let us confine ourselves to the chief thought: prayer as an appeal to the friendship of God; and we shall find that two lessons are specially suggested. The one, that if we are God's friends and come as such to Him we must prove ourselves the friends of the needy; God's friendship to us and ours to others go hand in hand. The other, that when we come thus we may use the utmost liberty in claiming an answer.

There is a twofold use of prayer: the one, to obtain strength and blessing for our own life; the other, the higher, the true glory of prayer, for which Christ has taken us into His fellowship and teaching, is intercession, where prayer is the royal power a child of God exercises in heaven on behalf of others and even of the kingdom. We see it in Scripture how it was in intercession for others that Abraham and Moses, Samuel and Elijah, with all the holy men of old, proved that they had power with God and prevailed. It is when we give ourselves to be a blessing that we can specially count on the blessing of God. It is when we draw near to God as the friend of the poor and the perishing that we may count on His friendliness; the righteous man who is the friend of the poor is very specially the friend of God. This gives wonderful liberty in prayer. Lord! I have a needy friend whom I must help. As a friend I have undertaken to help him. In Thee I have a Friend, whose kindness and riches I know to be infinite: I am sure Thou wilt give me what I ask. If I, being evil, am ready to do for my friend what I can, how much more wilt Thou, O my heavenly Friend, now do for Thy friend what he asks?

The question might suggest itself, whether the Fatherhood of God does not give such confidence in prayer, that the thought of His Friendship can hardly teach us anything more: a father is more than a friend. And yet, if we consider it, this pleading the friendship of God opens new wonders to us. That a child obtains what he asks of his father looks so perfectly natural, we almost count it the father's duty to give. But with a friend it is as if the kindness is more free, dependent, not on nature, but on sympathy and character. And then the relation of a child is more that of perfect dependence; two friends are more nearly on a level. And so our Lord, in seeking to unfold to us the spiritual mystery of prayer, would fain have us approach God in this relation too, as those whom He has acknowledged as His friends, whose mind and life are in sympathy with His.

But then we must be living as His friends. I am still a child even when a wanderer; but friendship depends upon the conduct. 'Ye are my friends if ye do whatsoever I command you.' 'Thou seest that faith wrought with his works, and by works was faith made perfect; and the scripture was fulfilled which saith, And Abraham believed God and he was called the friend of God.' It is the Spirit, 'the same Spirit,' that leads us that also bears witness to our acceptance With God; 'likewise, also,' the same Spirit helpeth us in prayer. It is a life as the friend of God that gives the wonderful liberty to say: I have a friend to whom I can go even at midnight. And how much more when I go in the very spirit of that friendliness, manifesting myself the very kindness I look for in God, seeking to help my friend as I want God to help me.When I come to God in prayer, He always looks to what the aim is of my petition. If it be merely for my own comfort or joy I seek His grace, I do not receive. But if I can say that it is that He may be glorified in my dispensing His blessings to others, I shall not ask in vain. Or if I ask for others, but want to wait until God has made me so rich, that it is no sacrifice or act of faith to aid them, I shall not obtain. But if I can say that I have already undertaken for my needy friend, that in my poverty I have already begun the work of love, because I know I had a friend Who would help me, my prayer will be heard. Oh, we know not how much the plea avails: the friendship of earth looking in its need to the friendship of heaven: 'He will give him as much as he needeth.'

But not always at once. The one thing by which man can honour and enjoy his God is faith. Intercession is part of faith's training-school. There our friendship with men and

74

with God is tested. There it is seen whether my friendship with the needy is so real, that I will take time and sacrifice my rest, will go even at midnight and not cease until I have obtained for them what I need. There it is seen whether my friendship with God is so clear, that I can depend on Him not to turn me away and therefore pray on until He gives.

O what a deep heavenly mystery this is of perseverance prayer. The God who has promised, who longs, whose fixed purpose it is to give the blessing, holds it back. It is to Him a matter of such deep importance that His friends on earth should know and fully trust their rich Friend in heaven, that He trains them, in the school of answer delayed, to find out how their perseverance really does prevail, and what the mighty power is they can wield in heaven, if they do but set themselves to it. There is a faith that sees the promise, and embraces it, and yet does not receive it (Hebrews 11:13,39). It is when the answer to prayer does not come, and the promise we are most firmly trusting appears to be of none effect, that the trial of faith, more precious than of gold, takes place. It is in this trial that the faith that has embraced the promise is purified and strengthened and prepared in personal, holy fellowship with the living God, to see the glory of God. It takes and holds the promise until it has received the fulfilment of what it had claimed in a living truth in the unseen but living God.

Let each child of God who is seeking to work the work of love in his Father's service take courage. The parent with his child, the teacher with his class, the visitor with his district, the Bible reader with his circle, the preacher with his hearers, each one who, in his little circle, has accepted and is bearing the burden of hungry, perishing souls-let them all take courage. Nothing is at first so strange to us as that God should really require persevering prayer, that there should be a real spiritual needs-be for importunity. To teach it us, the Master uses this almost strange parable. If the unfriendliness of a selfish earthly friend can be conquered by importunity, how much more will it avail with the heavenly Friend, who does so love to give, but is held back by our spiritual unfitness, our incapacity to possess what He has to give. O let us thank Him that in delaying His answer He is educating us up to our true position and the exercise of all our power with Him, training us to live with Him in the fellowship of undoubting faith and trust, to be indeed the friends of God. And let us hold fast the threefold cord that cannot be broken: the hungry friend needing the help, and the praying friend seeking the help, and the Mighty Friend, loving to give as much as he needeth.

O my Blessed Lord and Teacher! I must come to Thee in prayer. Thy teaching is so glorious, and yet too high for me to grasp. I must confess that my heart is too little to take in these thoughts of the wonderful boldness I may use with Thy Father as my Friend. Lord Jesus I trust Thee to give me Thy Spirit with Thy Word, and to make the Word quick and powerful in my heart. I desire to keep Thy Word of this day: `Because of his importunity he will give him as many as he needeth.'

Lord! teach me more to know the power of persevering prayer. I know that in it the Father suits Himself to our need of time for the inner life to attain its growth and ripeness, so that His grace may indeed be assimilated and made our very own. I know that He would fain thus train us to the exercise of that strong faith that does not let Him go even in the face of seeming disappointment. I know He wants to lift us to that wonderful liberty, in which we understand how really He has made the dispensing of His gift dependent on our prayer. Lord! I know this: 0 teach me to see it in spirit and truth.

And may it now be the joy of my life to become the almoner of my Rich Friend in heaven, to care for all the angry and perishing, even at midnight, because I know my friend who always gives to him who perseveres, because of his importunity, as many as he needeth. Amen.

CHAPTER 9:
PRAYER PROVIDES LABORERS

"Then saith he unto his disciples, The harvest truly is 'plenteous, but the laborers are few. Pray ye therefore the Lord of the harvest, that he will send forth laborers into his harvest" (Matthew 9:37-38).

The Lord frequently taught His disciples that they must pray and how they should pray. But He seldom told them what to pray. This He left to their sense of need and the leading of the Spirit. But in the above scripture He expressly directs them to remember one thing. In view of the abundant harvest, and the need for reapers, they must cry to the Lord of the harvest to send laborers. Just as in the parable of the friend at midnight, He wants them to understand that prayer is not to be selfish; it is the power through which blessing can come to others. The Father is Lord of the harvest. When we pray for the Holy Spirit, we must pray for Him to prepare and send laborers for the work.

Why does He ask His disciples to pray for this? Could He not pray Himself? Would not one prayer of His achieve more than a thousand of theirs? Is God, the Lord of the harvest, not aware of the need? And would He not, in His own good time, send laborers without the disciples' prayers? Such questions lead us into the deepest mysteries of prayer and its power in the Kingdom of God. The answer to such questions will convince us that prayer is indeed a power on which the gathering of the harvest and the coming of the Kingdom do in very truth depend.

Prayer is no form or show. The Lord Jesus was Himself the truth; everything He spoke was the truth. It was when "He saw the multitude, and was moved with compassion on them, because they were scattered abroad, as sheep having no shepherd," that He called on the disciples to pray for laborers to be sent to them (see Matthew 9:36). He did so because He really believed that their prayer was needed and would help.

The veil which hides the invisible world from us was wonderfully transparent to the holy human soul of Jesus. He had looked long and deep and far into the hidden connection of cause and effect in the spiritual world. He had marked in God's Word how God called men like Abraham, Moses, Joshua, Samuel, and Daniel, giving them authority over men in His Name. God also gave these men the authority to call the powers of heaven to their aid as they needed them. Jesus knew that the work of God had been entrusted to these men of old and to Himself for a time here upon earth. Now it was about to pass over into the hands of His disciples. He knew that where they were given responsibility for this work, it would not be a mere matter of form or show. The success of the work would actual depend on them and their faithfulness.

As a single individual, within the limitations of a human body and a human life, Jesus feels how little a short visit can accomplish among these wandering sheep He sees around Him. He longs for help to have them properly cared for. He therefore tells His disciples to begin to pray. When they have taken over the work from Him on earth, they are to make this one of their chief petitions in prayer: that the Lord of the harvest Himself would send laborer into His harvest. But since He entrusted them with the work and made it to a large extent dependent on them, He gives them authority to apply to Him for laborers and makes the supply dependent on their prayer.

How little Christians really feel and mourn the need of laborers in the fields of the world, so ripe for the harvest. How little they believe that our labor supply depends on prayer and that prayer will really provide "as many as he needeth." The dearth of labor is known and discussed. Efforts are sometimes made to supply the need. But how little the burden of the sheep wandering without a Shepherd is really assumed in the faith that the Lord of the harvest will send forth the laborers in answer to prayer. Without this prayer, fields ready for reaping will be left to perish. And yet it is so. The Lord has surrendered His work to His Church. He has made Himself dependent on them as His Body, through whom His work must be done. The power which the Lord gives His people to exercise in heaven and earth is real; the number of laborers and the measure of the harvest does actually depend on their prayer.

Why don't we obey the Master's instruction more heartily

and cry more earnestly for laborers? There are two reasons. The one is: We miss the compassion of Jesus which gave rise to this request for prayer. Believers must learn to love their neighbors as themselves and to live entirely for God's glory in their relationships with fellow-men. The Father's first commandment to His redeemed ones is that they accept those who are perishing as the charge entrusted to them by their Lord. Accept them not only as a field of labor, but as the objects of loving care and interest. Soon, compassion towards the hopelessly perishing will touch your heart, and the cry will ascend with a new sincerity.

The other reason for the neglect of the command is: We believe too little in the power of prayer to bring about definite results. We do not live close enough to God to be capable of the confidence that He will answer. We have not surrendered entirely to His service and Kingdom. But our lack of faith will be overcome as we plead for help. Let us pray for a life in union with Christ, so that His compassion streams into us and His Spirit assures us that our prayer is heard.

Such prayer will obtain a twofold blessing. There will first be a desire for an increase in the number of men entirely given up to the service of God. That there are times when men actually cannot be found for the service of the Master as ministers, missionaries, or teachers of God's Word is a terrible blot upon the Church of Christ. As God's children make this a matter of supplication in their own circles or churches, it will be given. The Lord Jesus is now Lord of the harvest. He has been exalted to bestow the gifts of the Spirit. He wants to make gifts of men filled with the Spirit. But His supply and distribution of these gifts depend on the cooperation of the members with Him. Prayer will lead to such cooperation and will stir those praying to believe that they will find the men and the means for the work.

The other blessing will be equally great. Every believer is a laborer. As God's children, we have been redeemed for service and have our work waiting. It must be our prayer that the Lord would fill all His people with the spirit of devotion, so that no one may be found standing idle in the vineyard. Wherever there is a complaint about the lack of fit helpers for God's work, prayer has the promise of a supply. God is always ready and able to provide. It may take time and importunity, but Christ's command to ask the Lord of the harvest is the pledge that the prayer will be heard. "I say unto you, he will arise and give him as many as he needeth."

This power to provide for the needs of the world and secure the servants for God's work has been given to us in prayer. The Lord of the harvest will hear. Christ Who taught us to pray this way will support the prayers offered ire His Name and interest. Let us set apart time and give all of ourselves to this part of our intercessory work. It will lead us into the fellowship of that compassionate heart of His that led Him to call for our prayers. It will give us the insight of our royal position as children of the King whose will counts for something with the great God in the advancement of His Kingdom. We will feel that we really are God's fellowworkers on earth, that we have earnestly been entrusted with a share in His work. We will become partakers in the work of the soul. But we will also share in the satisfaction of the soul as we learn how, in answer to prayer, blessing has been given that otherwise would not have come.

Lord, teach us to pray.

Blessed Lord! Once again You have given us another wondrous lesson to learn. We humbly ask that you let us see these spiritual realities. There is a large harvest which is perishing as it waits for sleepy disciples to give the signal for laborers to come. Lord, teach us to view it with a heart full of compassion and pity. There are so few laborers, Lord. Show us what terrible sin the lack of prayer and faith is, considering there is a Lord of the harvest so able and ready to send them forth. Show us how He does indeed wait for the prayer to which He has promised an answer. We are the disciples to whom the commission to pray has been given. Lord, show us how You can breathe Your Spirit into us, so that Your compassion and the faith in Your promise will rouse us to unceasing, prevailing prayer.

O Lord! We cannot understand how You can entrust such work and give such power to men so slothful and unfaithful. We thank You for all those whom You are teaching day and night to cry for laborers to be sent. Lord, breathe Your Spirit into all Your children. Let them learn to live only for the Kingdom and glory of their Lord and become fully awake to the faith in what their prayer can accomplish. And let our hearts be filled with the assurance that prayer offered in living faith in the living God will bring certain and abundant answer. Amen.

CHAPTER 10:
PRAYER MUST BE SPECIFIC

"And Jesus answered and said unto him, What would thou that I should do unto thee?" (Mark 10:51; Luke 18:41).

The blind man had been crying out loud repeatedly, "Thou Son of David, have mercy on me." The cry had reached the ear of the Lord. He knew what the man wanted and was ready to grant it to him. But before He did it, He asked him, "What wilt thou that I should do unto thee?" He wanted to hear not only the general petition for mercy, but the distinct expression of what the man's desire was that day. Until he verbalized it, he was not healed.

There are still petitioners to whom the Lord puts the same question who cannot get the aid they need until they answer that question. Our prayers must be a distinct expression of definite need, not a vague appeal to His mercy or an indefinite cry for blessing. It isn't that His loving heart does not understand or is not ready to hear our cry. Rather, Jesus desires such definite prayer for our own sakes because it teaches us to know our own needs better. Time; thought, and self-scrutiny are required to find out what our greatest need really is. Our desires are put to the test to see whether they are honest and real and are according to God's Word. We also consider whether we really believe we will receive the things we ask. Such reflective prayer helps us to wait for the special answer and to mark it when it comes.

So much of our prayer is vague and pointless. Some cry for mercy, but do not take the trouble to know exactly why they want it. Others ask to be delivered from sin, but do not name any sin from which a deliverance can be claimed. Still others pray for God's blessing on those around them-for the outpouring of God's Spirit on their land or on the world-and yet have no special field where they can wait and expect to see the answer. To everyone the Lord says, "What do you really want, and what do you expect Me to do?"

Every Christian has only limited power. Just as he must have his own specific field of labor in which to serve God, he must also make his prayers specific. Each believer has his own circle, family, friends, and neighbors. If he were to take one or more of these by name, he would find himself entering the training school of faith which leads to personal dealing with his God. When we have faithfully claimed and received answers in such distinct matters, our more general prayers will be believing and effectual. Not many prayers will reach the mark if we just pour out our hearts in a multitude of petitions, without taking time to see whether every petition is sent with the purpose and expectation of getting an answer.

Bow before the Lord with silence in your soul and ask such questions as these:

What is really my desire?

Do I desire it in faith, expecting to receive an answer?

Am I ready to present it to the Father and leave it there in His bosom?

Is there agreement between God and me that I will get an answer?

We should learn to pray in such a way that God will see, and we will know what we really expect.

The Lord warns us against the vain repetitions of the Gentiles, who expect to be heard because they pray so much. We often hear prayers of great earnestness and fervor, in which a multitude of petitions are poured forth. The Savior would undoubtedly have to respond to some of them by asking: "What do you want?"

If I am in a foreign country on business for my father, I would certainly write two different sorts of letters home. There will be family letters with typical affectionate expressions in them, and there will be business letters containing orders for what I need. There may also be letters in which both are found. The answers will correspond to the letters. To each sentence of the letters containing the family news I do not expect a special answer. But for each order I send I am confident of an answer regarding the forwarding of the desired article. In our dealings with God, the business element must be present. Our expressions of need, sin, love, faith, and consecration must be accompanied by an explicit statement of what we are asking for and what we expect to receive. In response, the Father loves to give us a token of His approval and acceptance.

But the word of the Master teaches us more. He does not say, "What dost thou wish?" but, "What dost thou will?" One often wishes for a thing without willing it. I wish to have a certain article but the price is too high, so I decide not take it. I wish, but do not will to have it. The lazy man wishes to be rich, but does not will it: Many people wish to be saved, but perish because they do not will it.

The will rules the whole heart and life. If I really will to have something that is within my reach, I do not rest until I have it. When Jesus asks us, "What wilt thou?" He asks whether it is our intention to get what we ask for at any price, however great the sacrifice. Do you really will to have it enough to pray continuously until He hears you, no matter how long it takes? How many prayers are wishes sent up for a short time and then forgotten! And how many are sent up year after year as a matter of duty, while we complacently wait without the answer.

One may ask if it wouldn't be better to make our wishes known to God, leaving it to Him to decide what is best, without our seeking to assert our wills. The answer is: by no means. The prayer of faith which Jesus sought to teach His disciples does not simply proclaim its desire and then leave the decision to God. That would be the prayer of submission for cases in which we cannot know God's will. But the prayer of faith, finding God's will in some promise of the Word, pleads for that promise until it comes.

In Matthew 9:28, Jesus said to the blind man, "Believe ye that I can do this?" In Mark He said, "What wilt thou that I should do?"(Mark 10:51). In both cases He said that faith had saved them. And He said to the Syrophenician woman, too, "Great is thy faith: be it unto thee even as thou wilt." Faith is nothing but the purpose of the will resting on God's Word and saying, "I must have it." To believe truly is to will firmly.

Such a will is not at variance with our dependence on God and our submission to Him. Rather, it is the true submission that honors God. It is only when the child has yielded his own will in entire surrender to the Father that he receives from the Father the liberty and power to will what he desires. Once the believer has accepted the will of God, as revealed through the Word and the Spirit, as his will, too, then it is the desire of God that His child use this renewed will in His service. The will is the highest power of the soul. Grace desires above everything to sanctify and restore this will to full and free exercise because it is one of the chief traits of God's image. God's child is like a son who lives only for his father's interests, seeks his father's will rather than his own, and is trusted by the father with his business. God speaks to that child in all truth, "What wilt thou?"

It is often spiritual sloth that, under the appearance of humility, professes to have no will. It fears the trouble of searching for the will of God, or, when found, the struggle of claiming it in faith. True humility is always accompanied by strong faith. Seeking to know only the will of God, that faith then boldly claims the fulfillment of the promise, "Ye shall ask what ye will, and it shall be done unto you."

89

Lord, teach us to pray.

Lord Jesus! Teach me to pray with all my heart and strength that there may be no doubt with You or with me about what I have asked. I want to know what I desire so well that as my petitions are being recorded in heaven, I can also record them here on earth and note each answer as it comes. Make my faith in what Your Word has promised so clear that the Spirit may work within me the liberty to will that it will come. Lord! Renew, strengthen, and sanctify my entire will for the work of effectual prayer.

Blessed Savior! I pray that You reveal to me the wonderful grace You show us, the grace that asks us to say what we desire and then promises to do it. Son of God! I cannot fully understand it. I can only believe that You have indeed redeemed us wholly for Yourself, and that You want to mold our wills, making them Your most efficient servant. Lord! I unreservedly yield my will to You as the channel through which Your Spirit is to rule my whole being. Let Him take possession of it, lead it into the truth of Your promises, and make it so strong in prayer that I may always hear Your voice saying, "Great is thy faith: be it unto thee even as thou wilt." Amen.

CHAPTER 11:
THE FAITH THAT TAKES

"Therefore I say unto you, All things whatsoever ye pray and ask for, believe that ye have received them, and ye shall have them" (Mark 11:24).

What a promise! It is so large, so Divine, that our little hearts cannot comprehend it. In every possible way we seek to limit it to what we think is safe or probable. We don't allow it to come in just as He gave it to us with its quickening power and energy. If we would allow it, that promise would enlarge our hearts to receive all of what His love and power are really ready to do for us.

Faith is very far from being a mere conviction of the truth of God's Word or a conclusion drawn from certain premises. It is the ear which has heard God say what He will do and the eye which has seen Him doing it. Therefore, where there is true faith it is impossible for the answer not to come. We must do this one thing that He asks of us as we pray: "Believe that ye have received. "He will see to it that He does the thing He has promised: "Ye shall have them. "

The essence of Solomon's prayer (2 Chronicles 6:4) is, "Blessed be the Lord God of Israel, who hath with His hands fulfilled that which He spake with His mouth to my father David." This should be the essence of all true prayer. It is the joyful adoration of a God whose hand always secures the fulfillment of what His mouth has spoken. Let us in this spirit listen to the promise Jesus gives because each part of it has a Divine message.

"All things whatsoever. "From the first word our human wisdom begins to doubt and say, "This can't possibly be literally true." But if it isn't, why did the Master say it? He used the very stongest expression He could find: "All things whatsoever." And He said it more than once: "If thou canst believe, all things are possible to him that believeth" (Mark 9:23); "If ye have faith as a grain of mustard seed... nothing shall be impossible to you" (Matthew 17:20). Faith is completely the work of God's Spirit through His Word in the prepared heart of the believing disciple. It is impossible for the fulfillment not to come, because faith is the pledge and forerunner of the coming answer.

"All things whatsoever ye shall ask in prayer believing, ye receive. " The tendency of human reason is to intervene here with certain qualifiers, such as "if expedient," "if according to God's will," to break the force of a statement which appears dangerous. Beware of dealing this way with the Master's words. His promise is most literally true. He wants His frequently repeated "all things" to enter our hearts and reveal how mighty the power of faith is. The Head truly calls the members of His Body to share His power with Him. Our

Father places His power at the disposal of the child who completely trusts Him. Faith gets its food and strength from the "all things" of Christ's promise. As we weaken it, we weaken faith.

The whatsoever is unconditional except for what is implied in the believing. Before we can believe, we must find out and know what God's will is. Believing is the exercise of a soul surrendered to the influence of the Word and the Spirit. Once we do believe, nothing is impossible. Let us pray that we do not limit Christ's "all things" with what we think is possible. Rather, His "whatsoever" should determine the boundaries of our hope and faith. It is seed-word which we should take just as He gives it and keep it in our hearts. It will germinate and take root, filling our lives with its fullness and bearing abundant fruit.

"All things whatsoever ye pray and ask for." It is in prayer that these" all things" are to be brought to God. The faith that receives them is the fruit of the prayer. There must be a certain amount of faith before there can be prayer, but greater faith is the result of prayer. In the personal presence of the Savior and in conversation with Him, faith rises to grasp what at first appeared too high. Through prayer we hold up our desires to the light of God's Holy Will, our motives are tested, and proof is given whether we are indeed asking in the Name of Jesus and only for the glory of God. The leading of the Spirit shows us whether we are asking for the right thing and in the right spirit. The weakness of our faith becomes obvious as we pray. But we are encouraged to say to the Father that we do believe and that we prove the reality of our faith by the confidence with which we persevere. It is in prayer that Jesus teaches and inspires faith. Whoever waits to pray, or loses heart in prayer because he doesn't feel the faith needed to get an answer, will never learn that faith. Whoever begins to pray and ask will find the Spirit of faith is given nowhere so surely as at the foot of the throne.

"Believe that ye have received." Clearly we are to believe that we receive the very things we ask. The Savior does not say that the Father may give us something else because He knows what is best. The very mountain that faith wants to remove is cast into the sea.

There is one kind of prayer in which we make known our request in everything, and the reward is the sweet peace of God in our hearts and minds. This is the prayer of trust. It makes reference to the countless desires of daily life which we cannot find out if God will give. We leave it to Him to decide whether or not to give, as He knows best.

But the prayer of faith of which Jesus speaks is something higher and different. Nothing honors the Father like the faith that is assured that He will do what He has said in giving us whatever we ask. Such faith takes its stand on the promise delivered by the Spirit. It knows most certainly that it receives exactly what it asks, whether in the greater interest of the Master's work or in the lesser concerns of daily life. Notice how clearly the Lord states this in Mark 11:23: "Whosoever shall not doubt in his heart, but shall believe that what he saith cometh to pass, he shall have it." This is the blessing of the prayer of faith of which Jesus speaks.

"Believe that ye have received." This word of central importance is too often misunderstood. Believe that you have received what you're asking for now, while praying! You may not actually see it manifested until later. But now, without seeing it, you are to believe that it has already been given to you by the Father in heaven. Receiving or accepting an answer to prayer is just like receiving or accepting Jesus. It is a spiritual thing, an act of faith separate from all feeling. When I go to Jesus, asking Him for forgiveness for a sin, I believe He is in heaven for just that purpose, and I accept His forgiveness. In the same way, when I go to God asking for any special gift which is according to His Word, I must believe that what I desire is mine. I believe that I have it; I hold it in faith; and I thank God that it's mine. "If we know that He hear us, whatsoever we ask, we know that we have the petitions that we desired of Him"(I John 5:15).

"And ye shall have them. "The gift which we first hold in faith as ours from heaven will become ours in personal experience. But will it be necessary to pray longer once we know we have been heard and have received what we asked? Additional prayer will not be necessary when the blessing is on its way. In these cases we should maintain our confidence, proving our faith by praising God for what we have received, even though we haven't experienced it yet.

There are other cases in which faith needs to be further tried and strengthened in persevering prayer. Only God knows when everything is fully ripe for the manifestation of the blessing that has been given to faith. Elijah knew for certain that rain would come. God had promised it. And yet he had to pray the seven times. That prayer was not just for show. It was an intense spiritual reality both in the heart of Elijah as he lay there pleading and in heaven where it has its effectual work to do. It is through faith and patience we inherit the promises (Hebrews 6:12). Faith says most confidently, "I have received it." Patience perseveres in prayer until the gift bestowed in heaven is seen on earth. "Believe that ye have received, and ye shall have. " Between the have received in heaven, and the shall have of earth, the key word is believe. Believing praise and prayer is the link. Remember that it is Jesus Who said this. As we see heaven opened to us and the Father on the throne offering to give us whatever we ask for in faith, we are ashamed that we have so little availed ourselves of the privilege. We feel afraid that our feeble faith will still not be able to grasp what is so clearly placed within our reach. One thing must make us strong and full of hope: It is Jesus Who brought us this message from the Father. He Himself lived the life of faith and prayer when He was on earth. When the disciples expressed their surprise at what He had done to the fig tree, He told them that the very same life He led could be theirs. They could command not only the fig tree, but the very mountain, and they would obey.

Jesus is our life. In us He is everything now that He was on earth. He really gives everything He teaches. He is the Author and the Perfecter of our faith. He gives the spirit of faith. Don't be afraid that such faith isn't meant for us. Meant for every child of the Father, it is within the reach of anyone who will be childlike, yielding himself to the Father's will and love and trusting the Father's Word and power. Dear fellow Christian!

Have courage! This word comes through Jesus, Who is God's Son and our Brother. Let our answer be, "Yes, blessed Lord, we do believe Your Word that we receive whatever we ask."

Lord, teach us to pray.

Blessed Lord! The Father sent You to show us all His Love and all the treasures of blessing that Love is waiting to bestow. Lord! You've given us such abundant promises concerning our liberty in prayer. We are ashamed that our poor hearts have accepted so little of it. It has simply seemed too much for us to believe.

Lord! Teach us to take and keep and use Your precious Word: "All things whatsoever ye ask, believe that ye have received." Blessed Jesus! It is in You that our faith must be rooted if it is to grow strong. Your work has completely freed us from the power of sin and has opened the way to the Father. Your love is longing to bring us into the full fellowship of Your glory and power. Your Spirit is constantly drawing us into a life of perfect faith and confidence. We are sure that through Your teaching we will learn to pray the prayer of faith. You will train us to pray so that we will believe that we really have what we ask for. Lord! Teach me to know and trust and love You in such a way that I live and dwell in You. Through You, may all my prayers rise up and go before God, and may my soul have the assurance that I am heard. Amen.

CHAPTER 12:
THE SECRET OF BELIEVING PRAYER

"Jesus, answering, saith unto them, Have faith in God. For verily I say unto you,... Whosoever shall not doubt in his heart, but shall believe that those things which he saith shall come to pass; he shall have whatsoever he saith" (Mark 11:22-23).

Answer to prayer is one of the most wonderful lessons in all Scripture. In many hearts it must raise the question, "How can I ever attain the faith that knows it receives everything it asks for?" It is this question our Lord will answer today.

Before He gave that wonderful promise to His disciples, Christ shows where faith in the answer to prayer originates and finds its strength. Have faith in God. This faith precedes the faith in the promise of an answer to prayer. The power to believe a promise depends entirely on faith in the promiser. Trust in the person engenders trust in what he says. We must live and associate with God in personal, loving communication. God Himself should be everything to us. His Holy Presence is revealed where our whole being is opened and exposed to

His mighty influence. There the capacity for believing His promises will be developed.

The connection between faith in God and faith in His promise will become clear to us if we consider what faith really is. It is often compared to the hand or the mouth, by which we take and use what is given to us. But it is important that we understand that faith is also the ear by which we hear what is promised and the eye by which we see what is offered. The power to take depends on this. I must hear the person who gives me the promise because the very tone of his voice gives me courage to believe. I must see him because the light of his face melts all my qualms about my right to take. The value of the promise depends on the promiser. It is on my knowledge of what the promiser is that faith in the promise depends.

For this reason Jesus says, "Have faith in God, " before He gives the wonderful prayer-promise. Let your eye be open to the living God. Through this eye we yield ourselves to God's influence. Just allow it to enter and leave its impression on our minds. Believing God is simply looking at God and what He is, allowing Him to reveal His presence to us. Give Him time and completely yield to Him, receiving and rejoicing in His love. Faith is the eye through which the light of God's presence and the vigor of His power stream into the soul. As that which I see lives in me, so by faith God lives in me, too.

Faith is also the ear through which the voice of God is always heard. The Father speaks to us through the Holy Spirit. The Son is the Word-the substance of what God says-and the Spirit is the living voice. The child of God needs this secret voice

100

from heaven to guide him, and teach him, as it taught Jesus, what to say and what to do. An ear opened towards God is a believing heart that waits to hear what He says.

The words of God will be not only the words of a book, they will be spirit, truth, life, and power. They will make mere thoughts come to life. Through this opened ear, the soul abides under the influence of the life and power of God Himself. As His words enter the mind, dwelling and working there, through faith God enters the heart, dwelling and working there.

When faith is in full use as eye and ear-the faculties of the soul by which we see and hear God-then it will be able to exercise its full power as hand and mouth-the faculties by which we take God and His blessings. The power of reception will depend entirely on the power of spiritual perception. For this reason, before Jesus gave the promise that God would answer believing prayer, He said, "Have faith in God." Faith is simply surrender. I yield myself to the suggestions I hear. By faith I yield myself to the living God. His glory and love fill my heart and have mastery over my life.

Faith is fellowship. I give myself up to the influence of the friend who makes me a promise and become linked to him by it. When we enter into living fellowship with God Himself, in a faith that always sees and hears Him, it becomes easy and natural to believe His promise regarding prayer. Faith in the promise is the fruit of faith in the promiser. The prayer of faith is rooted in the life of faith. And in this way the faith that prays effectively is indeed a gift of God. It is not something He bestows or infuses all at once, but is far deeper and truer.

It is the blessed disposition or habit of soul which grows up in us through a life of communion with Him. Surely for one who knows his Father well and lives in constant close communion with Him, it is a simple thing to believe the promise that He will do what His child wishes.

Because very many of God's children do not understand this connection between the life of faith and the prayer of faith, their experience of the power of prayer is limited. Sincerely desiring to obtain an answer from God, they concentrate wholeheartedly on the promise and try their utmost to grasp that promise in faith. When they do not succeed, they are ready to give up hope. The promise is true, but it is beyond their power to accept it in faith.

Listen to the lesson Jesus teaches us: Have faith in God, the Living God. Let faith focus on God more than on the thing promised, because it is His love, His power, His living presence that will awaken and work the faith. To someone asking to develop more strength in his hands and arms, a physician would say that his whole constitution must be built up. So the cure of feeble faith can be found only in the invigoration of our whole spiritual lives through communication with God. Learn to believe in God, hold on to God, and to let God take possession of our life. It will become easy to grasp the promise. Whoever knows and trusts God finds it easy to also trust the promise.

Note how distinctly this comes out in former saints. Every exhibition of the power of faith was the fruit of a special revelation from God. We see it in Abraham: "And the word of the Lord came unto Abram in a vision, saying, Fear not, Abram; I am thy shield .... And He brought him forth abroad, and said.....And he believed the Lord" (Genesis 15:1,5,6). And later again: "The Lord appeared to Abram, and said unto him, I am the Almighty God ....And Abram fell on his face, and God talked with him, saying, As for me, behold my convenant is with thee" (Genesis 17:1,3,4). It was the revelation of God Himself that gave the promise its living power to enter the heart and cultivate the faith. Because they knew God, these men of faith could not do anything but trust His promise. God's promise will be to us what God Himself is. The man who walks before the Lord and falls on his face to listen while the living God speaks to him will receive the promise. We have God's promises in the Bible with full liberty to claim them. Our spiritual power depends on God Himself speaking those promises to us. He speaks to those who walk and live with Him.

Therefore, have faith in God. Let faith be all eyes and ears. Surrender to God and let Him make His full impression on you, revealing Himself fully in your soul. Consider it a blessing of prayer that you can exercise faith in God as the living mighty God Who is waiting to give us the good pleasure of His will and faith with power. Regard Him as the God of love, Whose delight it is to bless and impart His love. In such faithful worship of God, the power will speedily come to believe the promise, too. "What things soever ye desire, when ye pray, believe that ye receive." Make God your own through faith; the promise will become yours, also.

Jesus is teaching us a precious lesson today. We seek God's

gifts, but God wants to give us Himself first. We think of prayer as the means of extracting good gifts from heaven, and we think of Jesus as the means to draw ourselves up to God. We want to stand at the door and cry. Jesus wants us to enter in and realize that we are friends and children. Accept His teaching. Let every experience of the weakness of our faith in prayer incite us to have and exercise more faith in the living God, and in such faith to yield ourselves to Him. A heart full of God has power for the prayer of faith. Faith in God fosters faith in the promise, including the promise of an answer to prayer.

Therefore, child of God, take time to bow before Him and wait for Him to reveal Himself. Take time to let your soul exercise and express its faith in the Infinite One in holy worship. As He shares Himself with and takes possession of you, the prayer of faith will crown your faith in God.

Lord, teach us to pray.

O my God! I do believe in You. I believe You are the Father, infinite in Your love and power. As the Son, You are my redeemer and my life. And as the Holy Spirit, You are my comforter, my guide, and my strength. I have faith that You will share everything You are with me and that You will do everything You promise.

Lord Jesus! Increase my faith! Teach me to take time to wait and worship in God's Holy presence until my faith absorbs everything there is in Him for me. Let my faith see Him as the fountain of all life, working with almighty strength to accomplish His will in the world and in me. Let me see Him in His love longing to meet and fulfill my desires. Let faith take possession of my heart and life to the extent that through it God may dwell there. Lord Jesus, help me! I want with my whole heart to believe in God. Fill me every moment with faith in God.

O my Blessed Savior! How can Your Church glorify You and fulfill the work of intercession through which Your Kingdom will come unless our whole lives consist of faith in God. Blessed Lord! Speak Your Word, "Have faith in God," into the depths of our souls. Amen.

CHAPTER 13:
PRAYER AND FASTING

"Then came the disciples to Jesus apart, and said Why could not we cast him out? And Jesus said unto them, Because of your unbelief. For verily I say unto you, If ye have faith as a grain of mustard seed, ye shall say unto this mountain, Remove hence to yonder place, and it shall remove; and nothing shall be impossible unto you. Howbeit this kind goeth nor out but by prayer and fasting" (Matthew 17:19-21).

When the disciples saw Jesus cast the evil spirit out of the epileptic whom they could not cure, they asked the Master why they had failed. He had given them "power and authority over all devils, and to cure all diseases." They had often exercised that power, and joyfully told how the devils were subject to them. And yet now, while He was on the Mount, they had utterly failed. Christ's casting the evil spirit out proved that there had been nothing in the will of God or in the nature of the case to make the miracle impossible. From their expression, "Why could we not?", it is evident that the disciples had wanted and tried to cast the spirit out. They had probably called upon it, using the Master's Name. But their efforts had been in vain. They had been put to shame in front of the crowd.

Christ's answer was direct and plain: "Because of your unbelief." Christ's success was not a result of His having a special power to which the disciples had no access. He had so often taught them that there is one power-the power of faith-to which, in the kingdom of darkness as in the Kingdom of God, everything must bow. In the spiritual world failure has only one cause: lack of faith. Faith is the one condition on which all Divine power can enter man and work through him. It is the sensitivity of man's will yielded to and molded by the will of God.

The power the disciples had received to cast out devils did not belong to them as a permanent gift or possession. The power was in Christ, to be received, held, and used by faith alone, living faith in Himself. Had they been full of faith in Him as Lord and Conqueror in the spirit world, had they been full of faith in Him as having given them authority to cast out in His Name, their faith would have given them the victory. "Because of your unbelief" was, for all time, the Master's explanation and reproof of impotence and failure in His Church.

Such a deficiency of faith must have a cause. The disciples may have asked, "Why couldn't we believe? Our faith has cast out devils before this. Why did we fail in believing this time?" The Master answers them before they can ask, "This kind goeth not out but by prayer and fasting."

Though faith is the simplest exercise of the spiritual life, it is also the highest. 'The spirit must yield itself in perfect receptivity to God's Spirit and become strengthened for this activity. Such faith depends entirely on the state of the spiritual life. Only when this is strong and in good health when the Spirit of God has total influence in our lives does faith have the power to do its mighty deeds.

Therefore Jesus adds, "Howbeit this kind goeth not out but by prayer and fasting." The faith than can overcome stubborn resistance such as you have just seen in this evil spirit, Jesus tells them, is not possible except for men living in very close fellowship with God and in very special separation from the world-in prayer and fasting. And so He teaches us two lessons in regard to prayer of deep importance. The one is that faith needs a life of prayer in which to grow and keep strong. The other is that prayer needs fasting for its full and perfect development.

Faith needs a life of prayer for its full growth. In all the different parts of the spiritual life there is a close union between unceasing action and reaction, so that each may be both cause and effect. Thus it is with faith. There can be no true prayer without faith; some measure of faith must precede prayer. And yet prayer is also the way to more faith: There can be no higher degrees of faith except through much prayer. This is the lesson Jesus teaches here.

Nothing needs to grow as much as our faith. "Your faith groweth exceedingly" is said of one church. When Jesus spoke the words,"According to your faith be it unto you" (Matthew 9:29), He announced the law of the Kingdom, which tells us

109

that different people have different degrees of faith, that one person may have varying degrees, and that the amount of faith will always determine the amount of one's power and blessing. If we want to know where and how our faith is to grow, the Master points us to the throne of God. It is in prayer, exercising one's faith in fellowship with the living God, that faith can increase. Faith can only live by feeding on what is Divine, on God Himself.

It is in the adoring worship of God-the waiting on Him and for Him in the deep silence of soul that yields itself for God to reveal Himself-that the capacity for knowing and trusting God will be developed. As we take His Word from the Blessed Book and ask Him to speak it to us with His living, loving voice, the power to believe and receive the Word as God's own word to us will emerge in us. It is in prayer, in living contact with God in living faith, that faith will become strong in us. Many Christians cannot understand, nor do they feel the need, of spending hours with God. But the Master says (and the experience of His people has confirmed) that men of strong faith are men of much prayer.

This brings us back again to the lesson we learned when Jesus, before telling us to believe that we receive what we ask for, first said,"Have faith in God." It is God-the living God-into Whom our faith must strike its roots deeply and broadly. Then it will be strong enough to remove mountains and cast out devils. "If ye have faith, nothing shall be impossible to you." If we could only give ourselves up to the work God has for us in the world! As we came into contact with the mountains and the devils that are to be cast away and cast out, we would soon comprehend how much we need great faith and prayer. They alone are the soil in which faith can be cultivated. Christ Jesus is our life and the life of our faith. It is His life in us that makes us strong and ready to believe. The dying to self which much prayer implies allows a closer union to Jesus in which the spirit of faith will come in power. Faith needs prayer for its full growth.

The second lesson is that prayer needs fasting for its full growth. Prayer is the one hand with which we grasp the invisible. Fasting is the other hand, the one with which we let go of the visible. In nothing is man more closely connected with the world of sense than in his need for, and enjoyment of, food. It was the fruit with which man was tempted and fell in Paradise. It was with bread that Jesus was tempted in the wilderness. But He triumphed in fasting.

The body has been redeemed to be a temple of the Holy Spirit. In body as well as spirit, Scripture says, we are to glorify God in eating and drinking. There are many Christians to whom this eating for the glory of God has not yet become a spiritual reality. The first thought suggested by Jesus' words in regard to fasting and prayer is that only in a life of moderation and self-denial will there be sufficient heart and strength to pray much.

There is also a more literal meaning to His words. Sorrow and anxiety cannot eat, but joy celebrates its feasts with eating and drinking. There may come times of intense desire, when it is strongly felt how the body and its appetites still hinder the spirit in its battle with the powers of darkness. The need is felt of keeping it subdued. We are creatures of the senses. Our minds are helped by what comes to us in concrete form. Fasting helps to express, to deepen, and to confirm the resolution that we are ready to sacrifice anything, even ourselves, to attain the Kingdom of God. And Jesus, Who Himself fasted and sacrificed, knows to value, accept, and reward with spiritual power the soul that is thus ready to give up everything for Him and His Kingdom.

There is still a wider application of Christ's words. Prayer is reaching out for God and the unseen. Fasting is letting go of everything that can be seen and touched. Some Christians imagine that everything that isn't positively forbidden and sinful is permissible to them. So they try to retain as much as possible of this world with its property, its literature, and its enjoyments. The truly consecrated soul, however, is like a soldier who carries only what he needs for battle. Because he frees himself of all unnecessary weight, he is easily capable of combatting sin. Afraid of entangling himself with the affairs of a worldly life, he tries to lead a Nazarite life as one specially set apart for the Lord and His service. Without such voluntary separation, even from what is lawful, no one will attain power in prayer. Such power comes only through fasting and prayer.

Disciples of Jesus!-You have asked the Master to teach you to pray, so come now and accept His lessons! He tells you that prayer is the path to faithstrong faith that can cast out devils. He tells you: "If ye have faith, nothing shall be impossible to you." Let this glorious promise encourage you to pray much. Isn't the prize worth the price? Give up everything to follow Jesus in the path He opens to us! Fast if you need to!

Do anything you must so that neither the body nor the world can hinder us in our great life-work-talking to God in prayer, so that we may become men of faith whom He can use in His work of saving the world.

Lord, teach us to pray.

O Lord Jesus! How continually You must reprimand us for our unbelief. Our terrible inability to trust our Father and His promises must appear quite strange to You. Lord! Let Your words, "Because of your unbelief," sink into the very depths of our hearts and reveal how much of the sin and suffering around us is our fault. Then teach us, Blessed Lord, that faith can be gained and learned in the prayer and fasting that brings us into living fellowship with Yourself and the Father.

O Savior! You are the Author and the Perfecter of our faith. Teach us what it means to let You live in us by Your Holy Spirit. Lord! Our efforts and prayers for grace to believe have been so ineffective. We know it is because we want You to give us strength in ourselves. Holy Jesus! Teach us the mystery of Your life in us-how You, by Your Spirit, live the life of faith in us, insuring that our faith will not fail. Make our faith a part of that wonderful prayer-life which You give to those who expect their training for the ministry of intercession to come from not only words and thoughts, but from the Spirit of Your own life. And teach us how, in fasting and prayer, we can mature in the faith for which nothing will be impossible. Amen.

CHAPTER 14:
PRAYER AND LOVE

"And when ye stand praying, forgive, if ye have ought against any; that your Father also which is in heaven may forgive you your trespasses" (Mark 11:25).

These words immediately follow the great prayer promise, "What things soever ye desire, when ye pray, believe that ye receive them, and ye shall have them" (Mark 11:24). We have already seen how the words that preceded that promise, 'Have faith in God,' taught us that, in prayer, everything depends: on the clarity of our relationship with God. These words that follow it remind us that our relationships: with our fellow-men must be clear, too. Love of God and love of our neighbor are inseparable. The prayer from a heart that is not right with God or with men will not succeed.

Faith and love are essential to each other. This is thought to which our Lord frequently gave expression. In the Sermon on the Mount, when speaking of the sixth commandment, He taught His disciples that acceptable worship of the Father was impossible if everything was not right with one's brother: "If thou art offering thy gift at the altar, and there rememberest that thy brother hath aught against thee, leave there thy gift before the altar, and go thy way; first be reconciled to thy brother, and then come and offer thy gift" (Matthew 5:23-24). After having taught us to pray, "Forgive us our debts, as we also have forgiven our debtors," Christ added, "If you forgive not men their trespasses, neither will your Father forgive your trespasses." At the close of the parable of the unmerciful servant, He applies His teaching in the words, "So likewise shall my heavenly Father do also unto you, if ye from your hearts forgive not every one his brother their trespasses" (Matthew 18:35).

Here, in Mark 11, beside the dried-up fig tree, as Jesus speaks of the power and the prayer of faith, He abruptly introduces the thought, "When ye stand praying, forgive, if ye have aught against any; that your Father also which is in heaven may forgive you your trespasses" (Mark 11:25). Perhaps the Lord had learned during His life that disobedience to the law of brotherly love was the great sin of even praying people, and the great cause of the ineffectiveness of their prayer. It is as if He wanted to lead us into His own blessed experience that nothing strengthens faith as much as the consciousness that we have given ourselves in love and compassion for those whom God loves.

The first lesson we are taught here is to have a forgiving disposition. We should pray, "Forgive us just as we have forgiven others." Scripture says, "Forgive one another, even as God also in Christ forgave you." God's full and free forgiveness should be the model of our forgiveness of men. Otherwise our reluctant, half-hearted forgiveness, which is not forgiveness at all, will be God's rule with us. All of our prayers depend on our faith in God's pardoning grace. If God dealt with us while keeping our sins in mind, not one prayer would be heard. Pardon open the door to all God's love and blessing. Because God has pardoned all our sins, our prayers can go through to obtain all we need.

The deep sure ground of answer to prayer is God's forgiving love. When it has taken possession of our hearts, we pray in faith. But also, when it has taken possession of our hearts, we live in love. God's forgiving nature, revealed to us in His love, becomes our nature. With the power of His forgiving love dwelling in us, we forgive just as He forgives.

If great injury or injustice occurs, try first of all to assume a Godlike disposition. Avoid the sense of wounded honor, the desire to maintain your rights, and the need to punish the offender. In the little annoyances of daily life, never excuse a hasty temper, a sharp word, or a quick judgment with the thought that we mean no harm, or that it is too much to expect feeble human nature to really forgive the way God and Christ do. Take the command literally: "Even as Christ forgave, so also do ye." The blood cleanses selfishness from the conscience. The love it reveals is a pardoning love that takes possession of us and flows through us to others. Our forgiving love toward men is the evidence of God's forgiving love in us. It is a necessary condition of the prayer of faith.

There is a second, more general lesson: Our daily life in the world is the test of our communication with God in prayer. How often the Christian, when he comes to pray, does his utmost to cultivate certain frames of mind which he thinks will be pleasing. He doesn't understand (or he forgets) that life does not consist of a lot of loose pieces which can be picked up at random and then be discarded. Life is a whole. The hour of prayer is only a small part of daily life. God's opinion of what I really am and desire is not based on the feeling I conjure up, but on the tone of my life during the day.

My relationship with God is part of my relationships with men. Failure in one will cause failure in the other. It isn't necessary that it be a distinct consciousness of something wrong between my neighbor and myself. An ordinary current of thinking and judging-the unloving thoughts and words I allow to pass unnoticed-can hinder my prayer. The effective prayer of faith comes from a life given up to the will and the love of God. Not as a result of what I try to be when praying, but because of what I am when I'm not praying, is my prayer answered by God.

All these thoughts can be gathered into a third lesson: In life among human beings, the one thing on which everything depends is love. The spirit of forgiveness is the spirit of love. Because God is love, He forgives. It is only when we are dwelling in love that we can forgive as God forgives. In love for our brothers we have the evidence of love for the Father, the basis for our confidence before God, and the assurance that our prayer will be heard. "Let us love in deed and truth; hereby shall we assure our heart before Him. If our heart condemn us not, we have boldness toward God, and whatever we ask, we receive of Him" (1 John 4:20; 3:18-22,23). Neither faith nor work will profit if we don't have love. Love unites us with God; it proves the reality of faith. "Have faith in God" and "Have love to men" are both essential commandments. The right relationships with the living God above me and the living men around me are the conditions for effective prayer.

This love is of special consequence when we are praying for our fellowmen. We sometimes commit ourselves to work for Christ out of zeal for His cause or for our own spiritual health, without giving ourselves in personal self-sacrificing love for those whose souls we seek. No wonder our faith is powerless and without victory! View each wretched one, however unlovable he is, in the light of the tender love of Jesus the Shepherd searching for the lost. Look for Jesus Christ in him and take him into a heart that really loves, for Jesus' sake. This is the secret of believing prayer and successful effort. Jesus speaks of love as the root of forgiveness. It is also the root of believing prayer.

There is nothing as heart-searching as believing prayer, or even the honest effort to pray in faith. Don't deflect that self-examination by the thought that God does not hear your prayer. "Ye ask and receive not, because ye ask amiss" (James 4:3). Let that Word of God search us. Ask whether our prayer is indeed the expression of a life completely given over to the will of God and the love of man. Love is the only soil in which faith can take root and thrive. Only in the love of fixed purpose and sincere obedience can faith obtain the blessing. Whoever gives himself to let the love of God dwell in him, whoever in daily life loves as God loves, will have the power to believe in the love that hears his every prayer. That almighty love is the Lamb Who is in the midst of the throne. It is suffering and enduring love that exists with God in prayer. The merciful shall obtain mercy; the meek shall inherit the earth.

Lord, teach us to pray.

Blessed Father! You are love, and only he who dwells in love can come into fellowship with You. Your blessed Son has taught me again how deeply true this. O my God! Let the Holy Spirit flood my heart with Your love. Be a fountain of love inside me that flows out to everyone around me. Let the power of believing prayer spring out of this life of love. O my Father! Grant by the Holy Spirit that this love may be the gate through which I find life in Your love. Let the joy with which I daily forgive whom ever might offend me be the proof that Your forgiveness is my power and life.

Lord Jesus! Blessed Teacher! Teach me how to forgive and to love. Let the power of Your blood make the pardon of my sins a reality, so that Your forgiveness of me and my forgiveness of others may be the very joy of heaven. Point out the weaknesses in my relationships with others that might hinder my fellowship with God. May my daily life at home and in society be the school in which strength and confidence are gathered for the prayer of faith. Amen.

CHAPTER 15:
THE POWER OF UNITED PRAYER

"Again I say unto you, That if two of you shall agree on earth as touching any thing that they shall risk, it shall be done for them of my Father which is in heaven. For where two or three are gathered together in my name, there am I in the midst of them" (Matthew 18:19-20).

One of the first lessons of our Lord in His school of prayer was not to pray visibly. Go into your closet and be alone with the Father. When He has taught us that the meaning of prayer is personal, individual contact with God, He gives us a second lesson: You also need public, united prayer. He gives us a very special promise for the united prayer of two or three who agree in what they ask. As a tree has its root hidden in the ground and its stem growing up into the sunlight, so prayer needs secrecy in which the soul meets God alone and public fellowship with those who find their common meeting place in the Name of Jesus.

The reason why this must be so is plain. The bond that unites a man with his fellow-men is no less real and close than that which unites him to God: He one with them. Grace renews not only our relationship with God, but our relationships with our fellow human beings, too. We not only learn to say "My Father." It would be unnatural for the children of family to always meet their father separately, never expressing their desires or their love jointly. Believers are not only members of one family, but of one Body. Just as each member of the Body depends on the other, the extent to which the Spirit can dwell in the Body depends on the union and cooperation of everyone. Christians cannot reach the full blessing God is ready to bestow through His Spirit until they seek and receive it in fellowship with each other. It was to the hundred and twenty praying together in total agreement under the same roof that the Spirit came from the throne of the glorified Lord. In the same way, it is in the union and fellowship of believers that the Spirit can manifest His full power.

The elements of true, united prayer are given to us in these words of our Lord. The first is agreement as to the thing asked. It isn't enough to generally; consent to agree with anything another may ask. The object prayed for must be some special thing,a matter of distinct, united desire. The agreement must be, as in all prayer, in spirit and in truth. In such agreement exactly what we are asking for becomes very clear. We find out whether we can confidently ask for it according to God's will, and whether we are ready to believe that we have received it.

The second element is the gathering in the Name of Jesus. Later, we will learn much more about the necessity and the power of the Name of Jesus in prayer. Here our Lord teaches us that His Name must be the center and the bond of the union that makes them one, just as a home contains and unites all who are in it. "The Name of the Lord is a strong tower: the righteous runneth into it, and is safe" (Proverbs 18:10). That Name is such a reality to those who understand and believe in it, that to meet within it is to have Him present. Jesus is powerfully attracted by the love and unity of His disciples: "Where two or three are gathered in my Name, there am I in the midst of them" (Matthew 18:20). The presence of Jesus, alive in the fellowship of His loving, praying disciples, gives united prayer its power.

The third element is the sure answer: "It shall be done for them of my Father." Although a prayer meeting for maintaining religious fellowship, or for our own edification, may have its use, this was not the Savior's reason for recommending it. He meant it as a means of securing special answer to prayer. A prayer meeting without recognized answer to prayer ought to be the exception to the rule. When we feel too weak to exercise the faith necessary to attain a distinct desire, we ought to seek strength in the help of others. In the unity of faith, love, and the Spirit, the power of the Name and the presence of Jesus acts more freely, and the answer comes more surely. The evidence that there has been true, united prayer is the fruit-the answer, the receiving of the thing for which we have asked. "I say unto you, It shall be done for them of my Father which is in heaven."

What an extraordinary privilege united prayer is! What a potential power it has! Who can say why blessing might be gained:

if the believing husband and wife knew they were joined

together in the Name of Jesus to experience His presence and power in united prayer (I Peter 33);

if friends were aware of the mighty help two or three praying in concert could give each other;

if in every prayer meeting the coming together in the Name, the faith in His presence, and the expectation of the answer stood in the foreground;

if in every church united, effective prayer were regarded as one of the chief purposes for which they are banded together;

if in the universal Church the coming of the Kingdom and of the King Himself were really matter of unceasing, united crying to God!

The Apostle Paul had great faith in the power of united prayer. To the Romans he writes, "I beseech you, brethren, by the love of the Spirit, that ye strive together with me in your prayer to God for me (Romans 15:30). He expects in answer to be delivered from his enemies and to prosper in his work. To the Corinthians he declares, "God will still deliver us, ye also helping together on our behalf by your supplications" (2 Corinthians 1:11). He expects their prayer to have a real share in his deliverance. To the Ephesians he writes, "With all prayer and supplication, praying at all seasons in the Spirit for all the saints and on my behalf, that utterance may be given unto me" (Ephesians 6:18-19). He makes the power and success in his ministry dependent on their prayers. With the Philippians he expects that his trials will become his salvation

124

and increase the progress of the gospel, "through your supplications and the supply of the Spirit of Jesus Christ" (Philippians 1:19). When telling the Colossians to continue praying constantly, he adds, "Withal praying for us too, that God may open unto us a door for the word" (Colossians 4:3). And to the Thessalonians he writes, "Finally, brethren, pray for us, that the word of the Lord may run and be glorified, and that we may be delivered from unreasonable men" (2 Thessalonians 3:1-2).

It is quite evident that Paul perceived himself as the member of a Body whose sympathy and cooperation he depended on. He counted on the prayers of these churches to gain for him what otherwise might not be given. The prayers of the Church were to him as real a factor in the work of the Kingdom as the power of God.

Who can say what power a church could develop and exercise if it would assume the work of praying day and night for the coming of the Kingdom, for God's power, or for the salvation of souls? Most churches think their members gather simply to take care of and edify each other. They don't know that God rules the world by the prayers of His saints, that prayer is the power by which Satan is conquered,and that through prayer the Church on earth has access to the powers of the heavenly world. They do not remember that Jesus has, by His promise, made every assembly in His Name a gate to heaven, where His presence is to be felt, and His power experience by the Father fulfilling their desires.

We cannot sufficiently thank God for the blessed work of

united prayer, with which Christendom, in our days, opens every year. It is of unspeakable value as proof of our unity and our faith in the power of united prayer, as a training school for the enlargement of our hearts to take in all the needs of the Church, and as a help to united persevering prayer. But it has been a special blessing as stimulus to continued union in prayer in the smaller circles. When God's people realize what it means to meet as one in the Name of Jesus, with His presenc in the midst of a Body united in the Holy Spirit, they will boldly claim the promise that the Father will do what they agree to request.

Lord, teach us to pray.

Blessed Lord! You ask so earnestly for the unity of Your people. Teach us how to encourage our unity with Your precious promise regarding united prayer. Show us how to join together in love any desire, so that Your presence is in our faith in the Father's answer.

O Father! We pray for those smaller circles of people who meet together so that they may become one. Remove all selfishness and self-interest, all narrowness of heart and estrangement that hinders their unity. Cast out the spirit of the world and the flesh through which Your promise loses all its power. Let the thought of Your presence and the Father's favor draw us all nearer to each other.

Grant especially, blessed Lord, that Your Church may believe that it is by the power of united prayer that she can bind and loose in heaven, cast out Satan, save souls, remove mountains, and hasten the coming of the Kingdom. And grant, good Lord, that my prayer circle may indeed pray with the power through which Your Name and Word are glorified. Amen.

CHAPTER 16:
THE POWER OF
PERSEVERING PRAYER

"And he spake a parable unto them to this end, that men ought always to pray, and not to faint; saying there was in a city a judge, which feared not God neither regarded man: And there was a widow in that city; and she came unto him, saying, Avenge me of mine adversary. And he would not for a while but afterward he said within himself, Though I fear not God, nor regard man; Yet because this widow troubleth me, I will avenge her, lest by her continual coming she weary me. And the Lord said, Hear what the unjust judge saith. And shall not God avenge his own elect, which cry day and night unto him, though he bear long with them? I tell you that he will avenge them speedily. Nevertheless, when the Son of may cometh, shall he find faith on the earth?" (Luke18:1-8).

Of all the mysteries of the prayer world, the need for persevering prayer is one of the greatest. We cannot easily understand why the Lord, Who is so loving and longing to bless us, should have to be petitioned time after time, sometimes year after year, before the answer comes. It is also one of the greatest practical difficulties in the exercise of believing prayer. When our repeated prayers remain unanswered, it is easy for our lazy flesh maintaining the appearance of pious submission- to think that we must stop praying because God may have a secret reason for withholding His answer to our request. Faith alone can overcome difficulty. Once faith has taken its stand on God's Word and the Name of Jesus, and has yielded itself to the leading of the Spirit to seek only God's will and honor in its prayer, it need not be discouraged by delay. It knows from Scripture that the power of believing, prayer is considerable; real faith can never be disappointed. It knows that to exercise its power, it must he gathered up, just like water, until the stream carp come down in full force. Prayer must often be "heaped up" until God sees that its measure is full. Then the answer comes. Just as each of ten thousand seeds is a part of the final harvest, frequently be repeated, persevering prayer is necessary to acquire a desired blessing. Every single believing prayer has its influence. It is stored up toward an answer which comes in due time to whomever perseveres to the end. Human thoughts and possibilities have nothing to do with it; only the Word of the living God matters. Abraham for so long "in hope believed against hope" and then "through faith and patience inherited the promise." Wait and pray often for the coming of the Lord to fulfill His promise.

When the answer to our prayer does not come at once we should combine quiet patience and joyful as confidence in our persevering prayer. To enable us to do this, we must try to understand two words in which our Lord describes the character and conduct of our God and Father towards those who cry day and night to Him: "He is long-suffering over them. He will avenge them speedily."

The Master uses the word speedily. The blessing is all prepared. The Father is not only willing, but most anxious to give them what they ask. His everlasting love burns with His longing desire to reveal itself fully to His beloved and to satisfy their need. God will not delay one moment longer than is absolutely necessary. He will do everything in His power to hasten the answer.

But why-if this is true and God's power is infinite does it often take so long to get an answer to prayer? And why must God's own elect so often, in the midst of suffering and conflict, cry day an night? "He is long-suffering over them." "Behold! the husbandman waiteth for the precious fruit of the earth, being long-suffering over it, till he receive the early and the latter rain" (James 5:7). Of course the husbandman longs for his harvest. But he knows it must have its full term of sunshine and rain, so he has plenty of patience. A child so often wants to pick the half-ripe fruit, while the farmer knows to wait until the proper time.

In his spiritual nature, man, too, is under the law of gradual growth that reigns in all created life. Only on the path of development can he reach his divine destiny. And only the Father, Who determines the times and seasons, knows the moment when the soul , or the Church is ripened to that fullness of faith in which it can really take and keep a blessing . As a father who longs to have his only child home from school, and yet waits patiently until the time of , training is completed, so it is with God and His children.

Insight into this truth should lead the believer to cultivate the corresponding attitudes of patience, faith, waiting, and praise, which are the secret of his perseverance. By faith in the promise of God, we know that we have the petitions we have asked of Him. Faith holds the answer in the promise as an unseen spiritual possession. It rejoices in it and praises God for it. But there is a difference between this kind of faith and the clearer, fuller, riper faith that obtains the promise as a present experience. It is in persevering, confident, and praising prayer that the soul grows up into full union with its Lord in which it can possess the blessing in Him.

There may be things around us that have to be corrected through prayer before the answer can fully happen. The faith that has, according to the command, believed that it has received, can allow God to take His time. It knows it has and must succeed. In quiet, persistent, and determined perseverance it continues in prayer and thanksgiving until the blessing comes. And so we see a combination of what at first sight appears to be so contradictory: the faith that rejoices in God's answer as a present possession combined with the patience that cries day and night until that answer comes. The waiting child meets God triumphantly with his patient faith.

The great danger in this school is the temptation to think that it may not be God's will to give us what we desire. If our prayer agrees with God's Word and is led by the Spirit, don't give way to these fears.

Learn to give God time. He needs time with us. In daily fellowship with Him, we must give Him time to exercise the full influence of His presence in us. Day by day, as we are kept waiting, it is necessary that faith be given time to prove its reality and fill our beings entirely. God will lead us from faith to vision; we will see His glory.

Don't let delay shake your faith, for it is faith that will provide the answer in time. Each believing prayer is a step nearer to the final victory! It ripens the fruit, conquers hindrances in the unseen world, and hastens the end. Child of God! Give the Father time! He is long-suffering over you. He wants your blessing to be rich, full, and sure. Give Him time, but continue praying day and night. And above all, remember the promise: "I say unto you, He will avenge them speedily."

The blessing of such persevering prayer is indescribable. There is nothing that examines the heart more closely than the prayer of faith. It teaches you to discover, confess, and give up everything that hinders the coming of the blessing everything that is not in accordance with the Father's will. It leads to closer fellowship with Him, Who alone can teach you to pray. Complete surrender becomes possible under the covering of the blood and the Spirit. Christian! Give God time! He will perfect whatever concerns you!

Let your attitude be the same whether you are praying for yourself or for others. All labor, bodily or mental, needs time and effort. We must give ourselves up to it. Nature reveals her secrets and yields her treasures only to diligent and thoughtful labor. However little we can understand it, spiritual husbandry is always the same: The seed we sow in the soil of heaven, the efforts we put forth, and the influence we seek to exert in the world above all require our complete surrender in prayer. Maintain great confidence that when the time is right, we will reap abundantly if we don't give up (Galatians 6:9).

Let us especially learn this lesson as we pray for the Church of Christ. She is indeed like a poor widow in the absence of her Lord, apparently at the mercy of her adversary and helpless to correct the situation. When we pray for His Church or any portion of it that is under the power of the world, let us ask Him to visit her with mighty workings of His Spirit to prepare her for His coming. Pray in the assured faith that prayer does help. Unceasing prayer will bring the answer. Just give God time. And remember this day and night: "Hear what the unrighteous judge saith. And shall not God avenge His own elect, which cry to Him day and night, and He is longsuffering over them. I say unto you, He will avenge them speedily."

Lord, teach us to pray.

O Lord my God! Teach me how to know Your way and in faith to learn what Your beloved Son has taught: "He will avenge them speedily." Let Your tender love, and the delight You have in hearing and blessing Your children, lead me implicitly to accept the promise that we may have whatever we ask for, and that the answer will be seen in due time. Lord! We understand nature's seasons; we know how to wait for the fruit we long for. Fill us with the assurance that You won't delay one moment longer than is necessary, and that our faith will hasten the answer.

Blessed Master! You have said that God's elect appeal to Him day and night. Please teach us to understand this. You know how quickly we become tired. Perhaps we feel that the Divine Majesty of the Father is so far beyond the reach of our continued prayer that is isn't becoming for us to plead with Him too much. O Lord! Teach me how real the labor of prayer is! I know that here on earth, when I fail at something, I can often succeed by renewed and more continuous effort, and by taking more time and thought. Show me how, by giving myself more entirely to prayer-by actually living in prayer I can obtain what I have asked for.

Above all, O blessed Teacher, Author and Perfecter of my faith, let my whole life be one of faith in the Son of God Who loved me and gave Himself for me! In You my prayer gains acceptance and I have the assurance of the answer. Lord Jesus! In such faith I will pray always, ceasing never. Amen.

AUTHOR'S NOTE

The need of persevering prayer appears to be at variance with the faith which knows that it has received what it asks (Mark 11:24). One of the mysteries of the Divine life is the harmony between sudden, complete possession and slow, imperfect appropriation. Here persevering prayer appears to be the school in which the soul is strengthened for the boldness of faith. Considering the diversity of operations of the Spirit, there may be some in whom faith takes the form of persistent waiting. For others, triumphant thanksgiving appears the only proper expression of the assurance of having been heard.

CHAPTER 17:
PRAYER IN HARMONY WITH GOD

"Father, I thank thee that thou hast heard me. And I knew that thou hearest me always" (John 11:41-42).

"Thou art my Son; this day have I begotten thee. Ask of me, and I shall give thee" (Psalm 2:7-8).

In the New Testament we find a distinction made between faith and knowledge. "To one is given, through the Spirit, the word of wisdom; to another the word of knowledge, according to the same Spirit; to another faith, in the same Spirit" (1 Corinthians 12:8-9). In a child or an uninformed Christian there may be much faith with little knowledge. Childlike simplicity accepts the truth without difficulty, and often cares little to give any reason for its faith but this: God said it. But it is the will of God that we should love and serve Him, not only with all the heart but also with all the mind. He wants us to develop an insight into the Divine wisdom and beauty of all His ways, words, and works. Only in this way will the believer be able to fully approach and rightly adore the glory of God's grace. And only thus can our hearts intelligently understand the treasures of wisdom and knowledge, that exist in redemption, preparing us to join in the,highest note of the song that rises before the throne: "O the depth of the riches both of the wisdom and knowledge of God!"

This truth has its full application in our prayer life. While prayer and faith are so simple that the newborn convert can pray with power, more mature Christians may find in the doctrine of prayer some of their deepest questions. How extensive is the power of prayer? How can God grant to prayer such mighty power? How can prayer be harmonized with the will of God? How can God's sovereignty and our will God's liberty and ours-be reconciled? These and similar questions are appropriate subjects for Christian meditation and inquiry. The more earnestly and reverently we approach such mysteries, the more we will fall down in adoring wonder to praise Him Who has in prayer given such power to man.

One of the difficulties with regard to prayer is the result of the perfection of God. He is absolutely independent of everything outside of Himself. He is an infinite being Who owes what He is to Himself alone. With His wise and holy will, He has determined Himself and everything that is to be. How can our prayer influence Him? How can He be moved by prayer to do what He otherwise would not do? Isn't the promise of an answer to prayer simply a condescension to our weakness? Is the power of prayer anything more than an accommodation of our mode of thought, because the accomplishments of Deity are never dependent of any outside action? And isn't the real blessing of prayer simply the influence it exerts on us?

Seeking answers to such questions provides the key to the very being of God in the mystery of the Holy Trinity. If God were only one Person, shut up within Himself, there could be no thought of nearness to Him or influence on Him. But in God there are three Persons: Father and Son, Who have in the Holy Spirit their living bond of unity and fellowship. When the Father gave the Son a place next to Himself as His equal and His counselor, He opened a way for prayer and its influence into the very inmost life of Deity itself.

On earth, just as in heaven, the whole relationship between Father and Son is that of giving and taking. If the taking is to be as voluntary and self-determined as the giving, the Son must ask and receive. "Thou art my Son; this day I have begotten thee. Ask of me, and I shall give thee" (Psalm 2:7-8). The Father gave the Son the place and the power to influence Him. The Son's asking wasn't just for show. It was one of those life-movements in which the love of the Father and the Son met and completed each other. The Father had determined that He would not be alone in His counsels. Their fulfillment would depend on the Son's asking and receiving. Thus asking was in the very Being and Life of God. Prayer on earth was to be the reflection and the outflow of this.

Jesus said, "I knew that Thou hearest me always" (John 11:42). Just as the Sonship of Jesus on earth cannot be separated from His Sonship in heaven, His prayer on earth is the continuation and the counterpart of His asking in heaven. His prayer is the link between the eternal asking of the only begotten Son in the bosom of the Father and the prayer of men on earth. Prayer has its rise and its deepest source in the very Being of God. In the bosom of Deity nothing is ever done without prayer-the asking of the Son and the giving of the Father.

This may help us to understand how the prayer of man, coming through the Son, can have an effect on God. God's decrees are not made without reference to the Son, His petition, or a petition sent up through Him. The Lord Jesus is the first-begotten, the Head and Heir of all things. As the Representative of all creation, He always has a voice in the Father's decisions. In the decrees of the eternal purpose, room was always left for the liberty of the Son as Mediator and Intercessor. The same holds true for the petitions of all who draw near to the Father through the Son.

If Christ's liberty and power to influence the Father seems to be at variance with the immutability of the Divine decrees, remember that God doesn't leave a past, as man does, to which He is irrevocably bound. The distinctions of time have no meaning to Him Who inhabits eternity. Eternity is an everpresent now, in which the past never passes and the future is always present. To meet our human comprehension of time, Scripture must speak of past decrees and a coming future.

In reality, the unchanging nature of God's plan is still in perfect harmony with His liberty to do whatever He wills. The prayers of the Son and His people weren't included in the eternal decrees simply for show. Rather, the Father listens with His heart to every prayer that rises through the Son. God really does allow Himself to be moved by prayer to do what He otherwise would not have done.

This perfect, harmonious union of Divine sovereignty and human liberty is an unfathomable mystery because God as the Eternal One transcends all our thoughts. But let it be our comfort and strength to know that in the eternal fellowship of the Father and the Son, the power of prayer has its origin and certainty. Through our union with the Son, our prayer is taken up and can have its influence in the inner life of the Blessed Trinity. God's decrees are no iron framework against which man's liberty struggles vainly. God Himself is living love, Who in His Son as man has entered into the tenderest relationship with all that is human. Through the Holy Spirit, He takes up everything human into the Divine life of love, leaving Himself free to give every human prayer its place in His government of the world.

In the light of such thoughts, the doctrine of the Blessed Trinity is no longer an abstract speculation, but the living manifestation of how man is taken up into the fellowship of God, his prayer becoming a real factor in God's rule of this earth. We can catch a glimpse of the light shining out from the eternal world in words such as these: "Through Him, we have access by one Spirit unto the Father."

Lord, teach us to pray.

Everlasting God! In deep reverence I worship before the holy mystery of Your Divine being. If it pleases You, most glorious God, to reveal some of that mystery to me, I would bow with fear and trembling rather than sin against You as I meditated on Your glory.

141

Father! I thank You for being not only the Father of Your children here on earth, but the Father of Jesus Christ through eternity. Thank You for hearing our prayers and for having given Christ's asking a place in Your eternal plan. Thank You also for sending Christ to earth and for His blessed communication with You in heaven. There has always been room in Your counsel for His prayers and the answers to those prayers. And I thank You above all that through Christ's true human nature on Your throne above, and through Your Holy Spirit in our human nature here below, a way has been opened by which every human cry of need can be received into the life and love of God, always obtaining an answer.

Blessed Jesus! As the Son, You have opened this path of prayer and assured us of an answer. We beseech You to teach us how to pray. Let our prayers be the sign of our sonship, so that we, like You, know that the Father always hears us. Amen.

CHAPTER 18:
PRAYER IN HARMONY WITH THE DESTINY OF MAN

"And he saith unto them, Whose is this image and superscription?" (Matthew 22:20).

"And God said, Let us make man in our image, after our likeness" (Genesis 1:26).

"Whose is this image?" It was with this question that Jesus foiled His enemies when they tried to trick Him, settling the matter of responsibility in regard to paying taxes. The question and the principle it involves are universally applicable, particularly to man himself. Bearing God's image decides man's destiny. He belongs to God and prayer to God is what he was created for. Prayer is part of the wondrous likeness he bears to His Divine original. It is the earthly likeness of the deep mystery of the fellowship of love in which the Trinity has its blessedness.

The more we meditate on what prayer is and on the wonderful power it has with God, the more we have to ask how man is so special, that such a place in God's plan has been allotted to him. Sin has so degraded him that we can't conceive of what he was meant to be based on what he is now. We must turn back to God's own record of man's creation to find what God's purpose was, and what capacities man was given to fulfill that purpose.

Man's destiny appears clearly in God's language at creation. It was to fill, to subdue, and to have dominion over the earth and everything in it. These three expressions show us that man was intended, as God's representative, to rule here on earth. As God's deputy, he was to fill God's place, keeping everything in subjection to Him. It was the will of God that everything done on earth should be done through man, i.e., the history of the earth was to be entirely in his hands.

In accordance with such a destiny was the position he was to occupy and the power at his disposal. When an earthly sovereign sends a representative to a distant province, that representative advises the sovereign as to the policy to be adopted there. The sovereign follows that advice, doing whatever is necessary to inact the policy and maintain the dignity of his empire. If the sovereign, however, doesn't approve of the policy, he replaces the representative with someone who better understands his desires for the empire. But as long as the representative is trusted, his advice is carried out.

As God's representative, man was to have ruled. Everything was to have been done according to his will. On his advice and at his request, heaven was to have bestowed its blessing on earth. His prayer was to have been the natural channel through which the Lord in heaven and man, as lord of this world, communicated. The destinies of the world were given into the power of the wishes, the will, and the prayers of man.

With the advent of sin, all this underwent a terrible change: Man's fall brought all creation under the curse. Redemption brought the beginning of a glorious restoration. In Abraham, God began to make Himself a people from whom kings (not to mention the Great King) would emerge. We see how Abraham's prayer power affected the destinies of those who came into contact with him. In Abraham we see how prayer is not only the means of obtaining blessing for ourselves. It is the exercise of a royal prerogative to influence the destinies of men and the will of God which rules them. We do not once find Abraham praying for himself. His prayers for Sodom and Lot, for Abimelech, and for Ishmael prove that a man who is God's friend has the power to control the history of those around him.

This had been man's destiny from the first. But Scripture tells us more: God could entrust man with such a high calling because He had created him in His own image and likeness. The external responsibility was not committed to him without the inner fitness. The root of man's inner resemblance to God was in his nature to have dominion, to be lord of all. There was an inner agreement and harmony between God and man, an embryonic Godlikeness, which gave man a real fitness for being the mediator between God and His world.

Man was to be prophet, priest, and king, to interpret God's will, to represent nature's needs, to receive and dispense

God's bounty. It was in bearing God's image that he could bear God's rule. He was indeed so much like God-so capable of entering into God's purposes and carrying out His plans that God could trust him with the wonderful privilege of asking for and obtaining what the world might need.

Although sin has for a time frustrated God's plans, prayer still remains what it would have been if man had never fallen: the proof of man's Godlikeness, the vehicle of his communication with the Father, and the power that is allowed to hold the hand that holds the destinies of the universe. Man is of Divine origin, created for and capable of possessing kinglike liberty. His prayer is not merely a cry for mercy. It is the greatest execution of his will.

What sin destroyed, grace has restored. What the first Adam lost, the second has won back. In Christ, man regains his original position, and the Church, abiding in Christ, inherits the promise: "Ask what ye will, and it shall be done unto you."

To begin with, such a promise does by no means refer to the grace or blessing we need for ourselves. It has reference to our position as the fruit-bearing branches of the heavenly Vine, who, like Him, only live for the work and glory of the Father. It is for those who abide in Him, who have forsaken themselves for a life of obedience and self-sacrifice in Him, who have completely surrendered to the interests of the Father and His Kingdom. They understand how their redemption through Christ has brought them back to their original destiny, restoring God's image and the power to have dominion.

Such men indeed have the power-each in his own area-to obtain and dispense the powers of heaven here on earth. With holy boldness they may make known what they will. They live as priests in God's presence. They are kings possessing the powers of the world to come. 1- {1- "God is seeking priests among the sons of men. A human priesthood is one of the essential parts of His eternal plan. To rule creation by man is His design.} They enter upon the fulfillment of the promise: "Ask whatsoever ye will, and it shall be done unto you."

Church of the living God! Your calling is higher and holier than you know! God wants to rule the world through your members. He wants you to be His kings and priests. Your prayers can bestow and withhold the blessings of heaven. In His elect who are not content just to be saved, but who surrender themselves completely, the Father will fulfill all His glorious counsel through them just as He does through the Son. In His elect, who cry day and night to Him, God wants to prove how wonderful man's original destiny was. Man was the image-bearer of God on earth, which was indeed given to him to rule. When he fell, everything fell with him. Now the whole creation groans and travails in pain together.

But now man is redeemed. The restoration of the original dignity has begun. It is God's purpose that the fulfillment of His eternal purpose and the coming of His Kingdom should depend on His people. They abide in Christ and are ready to accept Him as their Head, their great Priest-King. In their prayers they boldly say what they desire God to do for them. As God's image-bearer and representative on earth, redeemed man has the power to determine the history of this earth through his prayers. Man was created and then redeemed to pray, and by his prayer to have dominion.

"Priesthood is the appointed link between heaven and earth, the channel of communication between the sinner and God. Such a priesthood, insofar as expiation is concerned, is in the hands of the Son of God alone; insofar as it is to be the medium of communication between Creator and creature, is also in the hands of redeemed men-of the Church of God.

"God is seeking kings. Not out of the ranks of angels. Fallen man must furnish Him with the rulers of His universe. Human hands must wield the scepter, human heads must wear the crown." (The Rent Veil, by Dr. H. Bonar.)

Lord, teach us to pray.

"Lord! What is man, that thou art mindful of him? and the son of man, that thou visitest him? for thou hast made him a little lower than the angels, and hast crowned him with glory and honor. Thou madest him to have dominion over the works of thy lands; thou hast put all things under his feet .... 0 Lord our Lord, how excellent is thy name in all the earth!" (Psalm 8:4-6,9).

Lord God! Man has sunk so low because of sin. And how terribly it has darkened his mind. He doesn't even know his Divine destiny: to be Your servant and representative. How sad it is that, even when their eyes are opened, men are so unready to accept their calling! They could have such power with God and with men, too!

Lord Jesus! Through You, the Father has again crowned man with glory and honor; opening the way for us to be what He wants us to be. O Lord! Have mercy on Your people-Your heritage! Work mightily with us in Your Church! Teach Your believing disciples to accept and to go forth in their royal priesthood. Teach us to use the power of prayer to which You have given such wonderful promises, to serve Your Kingdom, to have rule over the nations, and to make the Name of God glorious on the earth. Amen.

CHAPTER 19:
POWER FOR PRAYING AND WORKING

"Verily, verily, I say unto you, He that believeth on me, the works that I do shall he do also; and greater works than these shall he do; because I go unto my Father. And whatsoever ye shall ask in my name, that will I do, that the Father may be glorified in the Son. If ye shall ask any thing in my name, I will do it" (John 14:12-14).

The Savior opened His public ministry in the Sermon on the Mount with the same subject He uses here in His parting address from the Gospel of John: prayer. But there is a difference. The Sermon on the Mount is directed to disciples who have just entered His school, scarcely knowing that God is their Father, whose prayers have reference chiefly to their personal needs. In His closing address, He speaks to disciples whose training time is coming to an end, who are ready as His messengers to take over His place and His work.

Christ's first lesson had been: Be childlike, pray believingly, and trust the Father to give you everything good. Here He points to something higher. The disciples are now His friends.

He has told then everything He knows about the Father. They are His messengers into whose hands the care of His work and Kingdom on earth is to be entrusted. Now they must assume that role, performing even greater works than Christ in the power of His approaching exaltation. Prayer is to be the channel through which that power is received. With Christ's ascension to the Father, a new epoch for both their working and their praying commences.

This connection comes out clearly in our text from John, chapter fourteen. As His Body here of earth, as those who are one with Him in heaven, the disciples are now to do greater works than He had done. Their successes and their victories are to be greater than His. Christ mentions two reasons for this. One is that He was going to the Father to receive all power; the other is that they could now ask for and expect that power in His Name "Because I go to the Father, and' (notice this and "and whatever ye shall ask, I will do." His going to the Father brings a double blessing: The disciple; could ask for and receive everything in His Name and as a consequence, would do the greater works This first mention of prayer in our Savior's parting words teaches us two most importantlessons. Whoever wants to do the works of Jesus must pray in His Name. Whoever prays in His Name must work in His Name.

In prayer the power for work is obtained. When Jesus was here on earth, He did the greatest works Himself. Devils that the disciples could not cast out fled at His word. When He went to be with the Fether, He was no longer here in body to work directly. The disciples were now His Body. All His work from the throne in heaven must and could be done here on earth through them.

Now that Christ was leaving the scene and could only work through commissioners, it might have been expected that the works would be fewer and weaker. He assures us of the contrary: "Verily, verily I say unto you, He that believeth on me, the works that I do shall he do also; and greater works than these shall he do; because I go unto my Father" (John 14:12). His approaching death was to be a breaking down of the power of sin. With the resurrection, the powers of the eternal life were to take possession of the human body and obtain supremacy over human life. With His ascension, Christ was to receive the power to communicate the Holy Spirit completely to His Body. The union-the oneness between Himself on the throne and those on earth was to be so intensely and divinely perfect, that He meant it as the literal truth: "Greater works than these shall he do, because I go to the Father."

And how true it was! Jesus, during three years of personal labor on earth, gathered little more than five hundred disciples, most of whom were so powerless that they weren't much help to His cause. Men like Peter and Paul did much greater things than He had done. From the throne He could do through them what He Himself in His humiliation could not yet do. He could ask the Father, receiving and bestowing new power for the greater works. And what was true for the disciples is true for us: As we believe and ask in His Name, the power comes and takes possession of us also to do the greater works.

Alas! There is little or nothing to be seen of the power to do anything like Christ's works, not to mention anything greater. There can only be one reason: the belief in Him and the believing prayer in His Name are absent. Every child of God must learn this lesson: Prayer in the Name of Jesus is the only way to share in the mighty power which Jesus has received from the Father for His people. It is in this power alone that the believer can do greater works. To every complaint about difficulties or lack of success, Jesus gives this one answer: "He that believeth on me shall do greater works, because I go to the Father, and whatsoever ye shall ask in my Name, that will I do." If you want to do the work of Jesus, believe and become linked to Him, the Almighty One. Then pray the prayer of faith in His Name. Without this our work is just human and carnal. It may have some use in restraining sin or in preparing the way for a blessing, but the real power is missing. Effective working first needs effective praying.

The second lesson is this: Whoever prays must work. It is for power to work that prayer has such great promises. Power for the effective prayer of faith is gained through working. Our blessed Lord repeats no less than six times (John 14:13-14; 15:7,16; 16:23-24) those unlimited prayer-promises which evoke anxious questions as to their real meaning: "whatsoever," "anything," "what ye will," "ask and ye shall receive."Many a believer has read these with joy and hope, and in deep earnestness of soul has attempted to plead them for his own need, arid has come out disappointed. The simple reason was that he separated the promise from its context.

The Lord gave the wonderful promise of the free case of His

Name with the Father in conjunction with doing His works. The disciple who lives only for Jesus' work and Kingdom, for His will and honor, vain be given the power to appropriate the promise. Anyone grasping the promise only when he wants something very special for himself will be disappointed, because he is making Jesus the servant of his own comfort. But whoever wants to pray the effective prayer of faith because he needs it for the work of the Master will learn it, because he has made himself the servant of his Lord's interests. Prayer not only teaches and strengthens one for work, work teaches and strengthens one for prayer.

This is true in both the natural and the spiritual worlds. "Unto every one which hath (more) shall be given" (Luke 19:26). Whoever is "faithful over a few things, I will make ....ruler over many things" (Matthew 25:21). With the small amount of grace we have already received, let us give ourselves to the Master for His work! It will be to us a real school of prayer. When Moses had to take full charge of a rebellious people, he felt the need, but also the courage, to speak boldly to God and to ask grea things of Him (Exodus 33:12,15,18). As you give yourself entirely to God for His work, you will feel that these great promises are exactly what you need and that you may most confidently expect nothing less.

Believer in Jesus! You are called-you are appointed -to do the works of Jesus, and even greater works He has gone to the Father to get the power to do them in and through you. Remember His promise "Whatsoever ye shall ask in my Name, that will I do. "Give yourself and live to do the works of Christ and you will learn how to obtain wonderful answers to prayer. You will learn to do not only what He did but much more. With disciples full of faith in Himself, boldly asking great things in prayer, Christ can conquer the world.

Lord, teach us to pray.

O my Lord! Once again, I am hearing You say things that are beyond my comprehension. I can do nothing but accept them and keep them in simple childlike faith as Your gift to me. You have said than because of Your going to be with the Father, anyone who believes in You can do not only the things You have done, but greater things as well.

Lord! I worship You as the Glorified One and eagerly await the fulfillment of Your promise. May my whole life be one of continued believing in You. Purify and sanctify my heart. Make it so tenderly susceptible to Yourself and Your love that believing in You will become its very breath.

You have said that because You went to the Father, You will do whatever we ask You to do. You want Your people to share Your power. From Your throne, You want to work through them, as members of Your Body, in response to their believing prayer in Your Name. You have promised us power in our prayers to You and power in our work here on earth.

Blessed Lord! Forgive us for not believing You and Your promise more. Because of our lack of faith, we have failed to demonstrate how You are faithful to fulfill that promise. Please forgive us for so little honoring Your all-prevailing Name in heaven or on earth.

Lord! Teach me to pray so that I can prove Your Name is all powerful with God, with men, and with devils. Teach me to work and to pray in a way that glorifies You, and do Your great works through me. Amen.

CHAPTER 20:
THE CHIEF END OF PRAYER

"I go unto my Father. And whatsoever ye shall ask in my name, that will I do, that the Father may be glorified in the Son" (John 14:12-13).

"'That the Father may be glorified in the Son': It is to this end that Jesus on His throne in glory will do everything we ask in His Name. Every answer to prayer He gives will have this as its object. When there is no prospect of this object being obtained, He will not answer. It follows as a matter of course that with us, as with Jesus, this must be the essential element in our petitions. The glory of the Father must be the aim-the very soul and life-of our prayer.

This was Jesus' goal when He was on earth: "I seek not mine own honor: I seek the honor of Him that sent me." In such words we have the keynote of His life. The first words of His High-Priestly prayer voice it: "Father glorify Thy Son, that Thy Son may glorify Thee. I have glorified Thee on earth: glorify me with Thyself" (John 17:1,4). His reason for asking to be taken up into the glory He had with the Father is a twofold one: He has glorified Him on earth; He will still glorify Him in heaven. All He asks is to be able to glorify the Father more.

As we begin to share Jesus' feeling on this point, ratifying Him by making the Father's glory our chief object in prayer, too, our prayer cannot fail to get an answer. The Beloved Son has said that nothing glorifies the Father more than His doing what we ask. Therefore, Jesus won't miss any opportunity to do what we request. Let us make His aim ours! Let the glory of the Father be the link between our asking and His doing!

Jesus' words come indeed as a sharp two-edged word, dividing the soul and the spirit, and quickly discerning the thoughts and intents of the heart. In His prayers on earth, His intercession in heaven, and His promise of an answer to our prayers, Jesus makes His first object the glory of His Father. Is this our object, too? Or are self-interest and selfwill the strongest motives urging us to pray? A distinct, conscious longing for the glory of the Father must animate our prayers.

The believer does at times desire it. But he doesn't desire it enough. The reason for this failure is that the separation between the spirit of his daily life and the spirit of his hour of prayer is too wide. Desire for the glory of the Father is not something we can arouse and present to our Lord when we prepare ourselves to pray. Only when the whole life in all its parts is given up to God's glory can we really pray to Christ's glory, too. "Do all to the glory of God," and "Ask all to the glory of God." These twin commands are inseparable. Obedience to the former is the secret of grace for the latter.

Living for the glory of God is the condition of the prayers that Jesus can answer.

This demand that prayer be to the glory of God is quite right and natural. Only the Lord is glorious. There is no glory but His, and what He allots to His creations. Creation exists to show forth His glory. Everything that doesn't glorify Him is sinful, dark, and dead. It is only in the glorifying of God that creatures can find glory. What the Son of Man did-giving Himself wholly to glorify the Father-is nothing but the simple duty of every redeemed one. He will also receive Christ's reward.

We cannot attain a life with God's glory as our only aim by any effort of our own. It is only in the man Christ Jesus that such a life can be found. Yes, blessed be God! His life is our life. He gave Himself for us. He is now our life. It is essential to discover, confess, and deny the self because it takes God's place. Only the presence and rule of the Lord Jesus in our hearts can cast out all self-glorification, replacing it with His own God-glorifying life and Spirit. It is Jesus, Who longs to glorify the Father in hearing our prayers, Who will teach us to live and to pray to the glory of God.

What power is there that can urge our slothful hearts to yield themselves to our Lord to work this in us? Surely nothing more is needed than a glimpse of how worthy of glory the Father is. Our faith should learn to bow before Him in adoring worship, ascribing to Him alone the Kingdom, the power, and the glory, yielding ourselves to life in His light. Surely we will be stirred to say, "To Him alone be glory." And we will look to our Lord Jesus with new intensity of desire for a life that refuses to recognize anything but the glory of God. When there isn't enough prayer to be answered, the Father is not glorified. It is our duty to live and pray so that our prayer can be answered. For the sake of God's glory, let us learn to pray well.

What a humbling thought it is, that so often there is earnest prayer in which the desire for our own joy or pleasure is far stronger than many desire for God's glory. No wonder there are so many unanswered prayers! Here we have the secret. God cannot be glorified when that glory is not the object of our prayers. Whoever wants to pray the prayer of faith must give himself to live literally so that the Father in all things is glorified in him. This must be his aim; without it there cannot be a prayer of faith.

"How can ye believe," said Jesus, "which receive honor of one another, and seek not the honor that cometh from God only?" (John 5:44). When we seek our own glory among men, we make faith impossible. Only the deep, intense self-sacrifice that gives up its own glory and seeks the glory of God wakens in the soul that spiritual susceptibility to Divine faith. The surrender to God and the expectation that He will show His glory in hearing us are essential. Only he who seeks God's glory will see it in the answer to his prayer.

How do we accomplish this? Let us begin with a confession. The glory of God hasn't really been an all-absorbing passion in our lives and our prayers. How little we have lived in the likeness of the Son and in sympathy with Him for God and

His glory alone. Take time to allow the Holy Spirit to reveal how deficient we have been in this. True knowledge and confession of sin are the sure path to deliverance.

And then let us look to Jesus. In death He glorified God; through death He was glorified with Him. It is by dying-being dead to self and living for God-that we can glorify Him. This death to self, this life to the glory of God, is what Jesus gives and lives in each one who can trust Him for it. Let the spirit of our daily lives consist of the decision to live only for the glory of the Father as Christ did, the acceptance of Him with His life and strength working it in us, and the joyful assurance that we can live for the glory of God because Christ lives in us. Jesus helps us to live this way. The Holy Spirit is waiting to make it our experience, if we will only trust and let Him. Don't hold back through unbelief! Confidently do everything for the glory of God! Our obedience will please the Father. The Holy Spirit will seal us within with the consciousness that we are living for God and His glory.

What quiet peace and power will be in our prayers when we know that we are in perfect harmony with Christ, Who promises to do what we ask, "That the Father may be glorified in the Son." With our whole beings consciously yielded to the inspiration of the Word and Spirit, our desires will no longer be ours. They will be His, and their main purpose will be the glory of God. With increasing liberty we will be able in prayer to say, "Father! You know we ask it only for Your glory. Answers to prayer, instead of being mountains we cannot climb, will give us greater confidence that we are heard. And the privilege of prayer will become doubly precious because it brings us into perfect unison with the Beloved Son in the wonderful partnership He proposes: "You ask, and I do, that the father may be glorified in the Son."

Lord, teach us to pray.

Blessed Lord Jesus! Once again I am coming to You. Every lesson you give me convinces me all the more deeply that I don't know hove to pray properly. But every lesson also inspires me with hope that You are going to teach me What prayer should be. O my Lord! I look to You with courage. You are the Great Intercessor. You alone pray and hear prayer for the sole purpose of glorifying the Father. Teach me to pray as You do.

Savior! I want to be nothing, yielding my totally to You. I am giving myself to be crucified with You. Through the Spirit the works of self will be made dead. Let your life and Your love of the Father take Possession of me. A new longing is filling my soul that every day and every hour prayer to the glory of the Father will become everything to me. O my Lord! Please teach me this!

My God and my Father! Accept the desire of Your child who has seen that Your glory is alone worth living for. Show me Your glory. Let it overshadow me and fill my heart! May I dwell in it as Christ did. Tell me what pleases You, fulfill in me Your own good pleasure, so that I may find my glory in seeking the glory of my Father. Amen.

CHAPTER 21:
THE ALL-INCLUSIVE CONDITION

"If ye abide in me, and my words abide in you, ye shall ask what ye will, and it shall be done unto you" (John 15:7).

In all God's relations with us, the promise and its conditions are inseparable. If we fulfill the conditions He fulfills the promise. What He is to be to us depends on what we are willing to be to Him: "Draw near to God, and He will draw near to you." Therefore, in prayer the unlimited promise, "Ask what ye will, " has one simple and natural condition, "if ye abide in me." It is Christ Whom the Father always hears. God is in Christ. To reach God, we must be in Christ, too. Fully abiding in Him, we have the right to ask whatever we want and the promise that we will get an answer.

There is a terrible discrepancy between this promise and the experience of most believers. How many prayers bring no answer? The cause must be either that we do not fulfill the condition, or God does not fulfill the promise. Believers are not willing to admit either, and therefore have devised a way of escape from the dilemma. They put a qualifying clause into the promise that our Savior did not put there-if it be God's will. This maintains both God's integrity and their own. If they could only accept it and hold fast to it as it stands, trusting Christ to make it true! And if only they would confess their failure in fulfilling the condition as the one explanation for unanswered prayer. God's Spirit would then lead them to see how appropriate such a promise is to those who really believe that Christ means it. The Holy Spirit would then make our weakness in prayer a mighty motivation for us to discover the secret and obtain the blessing of fully abiding in Christ.

"If ye abide in me. "As a Christian grows in grace and knowledge of the Lord Jesus, he is often surprised to find how God's words grow, too, into new and deeper meaning. He can look back to the day when some word of God was opened up to him, and he rejoiced in the blessing he had found in it. After a time, some deeper experience gave it a new meaning, and it was as if he never had seen what it contained. And yet once again, as he advanced in the Christian life, the same word stood before him as a great mystery, until the Holy Spirit led him still more deeply into its Divine fullness.

The Master's precious "Abide in me" is one of these evergrowing, never-exhausted words. Step by step, it opens the fullness of the Divine life to us. As the union of the branch with the vine is one of never-ceasing growth, so our abiding in Christ is a life process in which the Divine life takes more and more complete possession of us. The young believer may really be abiding in Christ to the limited extent which is possible for him. If he reaches onward to attain what the Master means by full abiding, he will inherit all the promises connected with it.

In the growing life of abiding in Christ, the first stage is that of faith. As the believer sees that Christ's command is really meant for him, his great aim is simply to believe that abiding in Christ is his immediate duty and a blessing within his reach. He is especially occupied with the love, power, and faithfulness of the Savior. He feels his one basic need is to believe.

It isn't long before he sees something more is needed. Obedience and faith must go together. But faith can't simply be added to obedience; it must be revealed in obedience. Faith is obedience at home, looking to the Master; obedience is faith going out to do His will.

The privilege and the blessings of this abiding are often of more interest than its duties and its fruit. Much self-will passes unnoticed. The peace which a young disciple enjoys in believing leaves him. In practical obedience the abiding must be maintained: "If ye keep my commands, ye shall abide in my love." Before, the truth that the mind believed was enough to let the heart rest on Christ and His promises. Now, in this stage, his chief effort is to get his will united with the will of his Lord, with his heart and life brought entirely under Christ's rule.

And yet there still seems to be something missing The will and the heart are on Christ's side; the disciple obeys and loves his Lord. But why does the fleshly nature still have so much power? Why aren't his spontaneous actions and emotions what they should be? Where is the beauty of holiness, the zeal of love, and the conformity with Jesus and His death, in which the life of self is lost? There must surely be something which he has not yet experienced through abiding in Christ.

Faith and obedience are just the pathway to blessing. Before giving us the parable of the vine and the branches, Jesus had very distinctly told what that full blessing is. Three times over He said, "If ye love me, keep my commandments," promising threefold blessing with which He would crown such obedient love: the indwelling of the Holy Spirit, the manifestation of the Son, the Father and Son coming to make Their abode within us.

As our faith grows into obedience, and in obedience and love our whole being reaches out and clings to Christ, our inner life opens up. The capacity is formed within us of receiving the life and the Spirit of the glorified Jesus, through a distinct and conscious union with Christ and with the Father. The word is fulfilled in us: "In that day ye shall know that I am in my Father and ye in me, and I in you" (John 14:20) God and Christ exist in each other, not only in will and in love, but in identity of nature and life. We come to understand that because of this union between the Father and the Son, so we are in Christ and Christ is in us in exactly the same way.

After Jesus had spoken thus, He said, "Abide in me, and I in you. Accept, consent to receive that Divine life of union with myself, in virtue of which, as you abide in me, I also abide in you, even as I abide in the Father. So that your life is mine and mine is yours." True abiding consists of two parts: occupying a position into which Christ can come and abide, and abiding in Him so that the soul lets Him take the place of the self to become our life. Like little children who have no cares, we find happiness in trusting and obeying the love that has done everything for us.

To those who thus abide, the promise, "Ask whatsoever ye will," comes as their rightful heritage. It cannot be otherwise. Christ has full possession of them. He dwells in their love, their wills, and their lives. Not only have their wills been given up, Christ has entered them, dwelling and breathing there by His Spirit. These people pray in Him. He prays in them, and the Father always hears Him. What they ask will be done for them.

Beloved fellow-believer! Let us confess that because we do not abide in Christ as He would like us to, the Church is impotent in the face of infidelity, worldliness, and heathendom. In the midst of such enemies, the Lord could make her more than a conqueror. We must believe that He means what He promises, and accept the conviction the confession implies.

But don't be discouraged. The abiding of the branch in the Vine is a life of never-ceasing growth. The abiding (as the Master meant it) is within our reach, for He lives to give it to us. Let us but be ready to count all things as loss and to say, "What I have attained so far is hardly anything. I want to learn to perceive Christ the same way He perceives me." It is not be occupied so much with the abiding as with Him to Whom the abiding links us and His fullness. Let it be Christ-the whole Christ, in His obedience and humiliation, in His exaltation and power,Whom our soul moves and acts. He Himself will fulfill His promise in us.

As we abide and grow into fuller and fuller abiding, let us exercise our right-the will to enter into God's will. Obeying what that will commands, let us claim what it promises. Let us yield to the teaching of the Holy Spirit. He will show each of us what the will of God is so that we may claim it prayer. And let us be content with nothing less than the personal experience of what Jesus gave when said, "If ye abide in me, ye shall ask what ye will, and it shall be done unto you."

Lord, teach us to pray.

Beloved Lord! Make Your promise in all simplicity new to men. Teach me to accept it, letting the only limitation on Your holy giving be my own willingness. Lord! Let each word of Your promise be, in a new way, made quick and powerful in soul.

You say, "Abide it? me!" O my Master, my Life my All-I do abide in You. Allow me to grow up in all your fullness. It is not the effort of faith, trying to cling to You and trusting You to protect me; nor my will, obeying You and keeping Your commandments, that alone can satisfy me. Only You Yourself, living in me as You do in the Father, can satisfy me. It is You, my Lord, no longer before me and above me, but united with me, that I need. I trust You for this.

You say, "Ask whatever you will."Lord! I know that a life of complete, deep abiding will renew, sanctify, and strengthen my will in such a way that I will have the desire and the liberty to ask for great things. Lord! Let my will-dead in Your death, living in Your life-be bold and large in its petitions.

You say, "It shall be done. "O Jesus! You are the Amen, the Faithful and True Witness. Give me in Yourself the joyous confidence that You will make this promise even more wonderfully true to me than ever before, because it has not entered into the heart of man to conceive what God has prepared for those who love Him. Amen.

AUTHOR'S NOTE

Many books and sermons on prayer emphasize the blessing of prayer as a spiritual exercise, even if there is no answer. God's fellowship ought to be more important to us than the gift we ask for. But a careful examination of what Christ said about prayer reveals that He wanted us to think of prayer more as the means to an end. The answer was to be the proof that we and our prayer are acceptable to the Father in heaven. It is not that Christ would have us consider the gifts of higher value than the fellowship and favor of the Father. By no means. But the Father intends the answer to be a token of His favor and of the reality of our fellowship with Him.

Daily answer to prayer is the proof of our spiritual maturity. It shows that we have attained the true abiding in Christ, that our will is truly one with God's will. It also reveals that our faith is strong enough to see and take what God has prepared for us, that the Name of Christ and His nature have taken full possession of us, and that we have been found fit to take a place among those whom God admits to His counsels, according to whose prayer He rules the world. Prayer is very blessed; the answer is more blessed still. It is the response from the Father that our prayer, our faith, and our will are indeed as He would wish them to be.

I make these remarks with the one desire of leading my readers to put together for themselves everything that Christ has said about prayer. Accept the truth that when prayer is what it should be, or rather when we are what we should be, the answer must be expected. It will bring us out from those refuges where we have comforted ourselves with unanswered prayer. It will show us the place of power to which Christ has appointed His Church, that place which it occupies so little. It will reveal the terrible weakness of our spiritual life as the cause of our not praying boldly in Christ's Name. It will urge us mightily to rise to a life in full union with Christ and in the fullness of the Spirit as the secret of effective prayer. And it will so lead us to realize our destiny: "At that day: Verily, verily I say unto you, If ye shall ask anything of the Father, He will give it you in my Name: ask, and ye shall receive, that your joy may be fulfilled." Prayer that is really, spiritually, in union with Jesus is always answered.

CHAPTER 22:
THE WORD AND PRAYER

"If ye abide in me, and my words abide in you, ye shall ask what ye will, and it shall be done unto you " (John 15:7).

The vital connection between the Word and prayer is one of the simplest and earliest lessons of the Christian life. As that newly-converted heathen put it: "I pray-I speak to my Father; I read-my Father speaks to me." Before prayer, God's Word strengthens me by giving my faith its justification and its petition. And after prayer, God's Word prepares me by revealing what the Father wants me to ask. In prayer, God's Word brings me the answer, for in it the Spirit allows me to hear the Father's voice.

Prayer is not monologue, but dialogue. Its most essential part is God's voice in response to mine. Listening to God's voice is the secret of the assurance that He will listen to mine. "Incline thine ear and hear," "Give ear to me," and "Hearken to my voice," are words which God speaks to man as well as man to God. His hearkening will depend on ours. My willingness to accept His words will determine the power my words have with Him. What God's words are to me is the test of what He

Himself is to me. It shows the uprightness of my desire to meet Him in prayer.

It is this connection between His Word and our prayer that Jesus points to when He says, "If ye abide in me, and my words abide in you, ye shall ask what ye will, and it shall be done unto you." The deep importance of this truth becomes clear if we notice the expression which this one replaces. More than once Jesus had said, "Abide in me and I in you. "His abiding in us was the complement and the crown of our abiding in Him. But here, instead of "Ye in me and I in you, "He says, "Ye in me and my words in you." The abiding of His words is the equivalent of Himself abiding.

What a view this opens up to us of the place the words of God in Christ are to have in our spiritual lives, especially in our prayer. A man's words reveal himself. In his promises, he gives himself away, binding himself to the one who receives his promises. In his commands, he proclaims his will, seeking to make himself master of those whose obedience he claims, to guide and use them as if they were part of himself. Through our words, spirit holds fellowship with spirit. If a man's words are heard, accepted, held fast, and obeyed, he can impart himself to someone else through them. But with human beings, this can happen only in a limited sense.

God, however, is the infinite Being in Whom everything is life, power, spirit, and truth, in the very deepest meaning of the words. When God reveals Himself in His words, He does indeed give Himself- love and His life, His will and His power to those who receive these words, in a reality passing comprehension. In every promise, He gives us the power to grasp and possess Himself. In every command, He allows us to share His will, His holiness, and His perfection. God's Word gives us God Himself. That Word is nothing less than the Eternal Son, Christ Jesus. Therefore, all of Christ's words are God's words, full of a Divine, quickening life and power. "The words that I speak unto you, they are spirit and they are life."

Those who study the deaf and mute tell us how much the power of speaking depends on that of hearing, and how the loss of hearing in children is followed by a loss of speaking, too. This is also true in a broader sense: Our speech is based on what we hear. In the highest sense, this is true of our conversation with God. To offer a prayer-to utter certain wishes and appeal to certain promises-is an easy thing that man can learn with human intelligence.But to pray in the Spirit-to speak words that reach and touch God, affecting and influencing the powers of the unseen world-depends entirely on our hearing God's voice. We must listen to the voice and language that God uses and, through the words of God, receive His thoughts, His mind, and His life into our hearts. The extent to which we listen will determine the extent to which we learn to speak in the voice and the language that God hears. The ear of the learner, wakened morning by morning, prepares him to speak to God. (Isaiah 1:4).

This hearing the voice of God is something more than the thoughtful study of the Word. One can study and gain knowledge of the Word having little real fellowship with the living God. But there is also a reading of the Word, in the very presence of the Father and under the leading of the Spirit, in which the Word comes to us in living power from God Himself. It is to us the very voice of the Father, a real, personal fellowship with Himself. The living voice of God enters the heart, bringing blessing and strength, and awakening the response of a living faith that reaches back to the heart of God.

The power both to obey and believe depends on hearing God's voice this way. The chief thing isn't knowing what God has said we must do, but that God Himself says it to us. Neither the law nor the book nor the knowledge of what is right works obedience. This can be accomplished only by the personal influence of God through His living fellowship. The presence of God Himself as the Promiser, not the knowledge of what He has promised, awakens faith and trust in prayer. It is only in the full presence of God that disobedience and unbelief become impossible.

"If ye abide in me, and my words abide in you, ye shall ask what ye will, and it shall be done unto you." In these words, the Savior gives Himself. We must have the words in us taken up into our wills and lives, reproduced in our inner natures and conduct. They must abide in us. Our lives must be one continuous display of the words that fill us. The words reveal Christ inside and our lives reveal Him outside. As the words of Christ enter our very hearts, becoming and influencing our lives, our words will enter His heart and influence Him. My prayer will depend on my life: Whatever God's words are to me and in me will determine what my words will be to God and in God. If I do what God says, God will do what I say.

The Old Testament saints understood this connection between God's words and ours quite well. Their prayer really was a loving response to what they had heard God speak. If the word were a promise, they counted on God to do as He had spoken. "Do as Thou hast said"; "For Thou, Lord, hast spoken it"; "According to Thy promise"; "According to Thy word": In such expressions they showed that what God spoke in promise was the root and the life of what they spoke in prayer. If the word was a command, they simply did as the Lord had spoken: "So Abram departed as the Lord had spoken." Their lives were fellowship with God, the exchange of word and thought. What God spoke they heard and did; what they spoke God heard and did. In each word, He speaks to us, and the whole Christ gives Himself to fulfill it. For each word, He asks no less than that we give the whole man to keep that word and to receive its fulfillment."If my words abide in you." The condition is simple and clear. In His words His will is revealed. As the words abide in me, His will rules me. My will becomes the empty vessel which His will fills, and the willing instrument which His will rules. He fills my inner being. In the exercise of obedience and faith, my will becomes stronger and is brought into deeper inner harmony with Him. Because He can fully trust it to will nothing but what He wills, He is not afraid to give the promise, "If my words abide in you, ye shall ask what ye will, and it shall be done unto you." To all who believe it and act upon it, He will make it literally true. Disciples of Christ! While we have been excusing our unanswered prayers with a fancied submission to God's wisdom and will, the real reason has been that our own feeble lives have been the cause of our feeble prayers! Nothing can make men strong but the word coming from God's mouth. By that we must live. The word of Christ makes us one with Him and fits us spiritually for touching and taking hold of God. We must love and live in that Word, letting it abide in and become part of us. All that is of the world passes away. Whoever does God's will lives forever. Let us yield heart and life to the words of Christ, the words in which He gives Himself, the personal living Savior. His promise will become our rich experience: "If ye abide in me, and my words abide in you, ye shall ask what ye will, and it shall be done unto you."

Lord, teach us to pray.

Blessed Lord! I see why my prayer has not been more believing and effective. I was more occupied with my speaking to You than with Your speaking to me. I did not understand that the secret of faith is this: There can be only as much faith as there is of the living Word dwelling in the soul.

Your Word taught me so clearly to be swift to hear and slow to speak, and not to be hasty to say just anything to God. Lord, teach me that it is only when I take Your Word into my life that my words can be taken into Your heart. Teach me that if Your Word is a living power within me, it will be a living power with You, also. Show me that what Your mouth has spoken Your hand will perform.

Lord Jesus! Deliver me from the uncircumcised ear! Give me the opened ear of the learner, wakened morning by morning to hear the Father's voice. Just as You speak only what You hear from the Father, may my speaking be the echo of Your speaking to me. "When Moses went into the tabernacle to speak with Him, he heard the voice of One speaking unto him from off the mercy seat." Lord, may it be so with me, too. Let my life and character reveal that Your words abide and are seen in me. May this be my preparation for the complete blessing: "Ye shall ask what ye will, and it shall be done unto you." Amen.

CHAPTER 23:
OBEDIENCE: THE PATH TO POWER IN PRAYER

"Ye have not chosen me, but I have chosen you, and ordained you, that ye should go and bring forth fruit, and that your fruit should remain; that whatsoever ye shall ask of the father in my name, he may give it you" (John 15:16).

"The effectual fervent prayer of a righteous man availeth much" (James 5:16).

The promise of the Father's giving whatsoever we ask is here once again renewed, showing us to whom such wonderful influence in the council chamber of the Most High is to be granted. "I chose you," the Master says, "and appointed you that ye should go and bear fruit, and that your fruit should remain." He then adds, to the end "that whatsoever ye," (the fruit bearing ones) "shall ask of the Father in my name, He may give it you." This is nothing but a fuller expression of what He meant by the words, "If ye abide in me." He had spoken of the object of this abiding as the bearing of "fruit," "more fruit," and "much fruit." In this, God would be glorified and the mark of discipleship would

181

be seen. He now adds that the reality of the abiding, as seen in fruit abounding and abiding, is the qualification for our praying so as to obtain what we ask. Entire dedication to the fulfillment of our calling is the key to effective prayer and the unlimited blessings of Christ's wonderful prayer-promises.

There are Christians who fear that such a statement is at variance with the doctrine of free grace. But surely it doesn't disagree with free grace rightly understood or the many express statements of God's blessed Word. Take the words of St. John, "Let us love in deed and truth; hereby shall we assure our heart before Him. And whatsoever we ask, we receive of Him because we keep His commandments, and do the things that are pleasing in His sight" (1 John 3:18-19,22). Or take the often-quoted words of James:"The effectual fervent prayer of a righteous man availeth much" (James 5:16). This describes a man of whom, according to the definition of the Holy Spirit, it can be said, "He that doeth righteousness, is righteous even as He is righteous." Mark the spirit of so many of the Psalms, with their confident appeal to the integrity and righteousness of the supplicant. In Psalm 18 David says: "The Lord rewarded me according to my righteousness; according to the cleanness of my hands hath he recompensed me... I was also upright before him, and I kept myself from mine iniquity. Therefore hath the Lord recompensed me according to my righteousness" (Psalm 18:20,23). See also Psalms 7:3-5; 15:1-2; 17:3,6; 26:16; 119:121, 153). If we carefully consider these scriptures in the light of the New Testament, we find them in perfect harmony with the explicit teaching of the Savior's parting words: "If ye keep my commandments, ye shall abide in my love"; "Ye are my friends if ye do what I command you." The words are indeed meant literally: "I appointed you that ye should go and bear fruit, that, "then, "whatsoever ye shall ask of the Father in my name, He may give it you."

Let us seek to enter into the spirit of what the Savior teaches us here. There is a danger in our evangelical religion of looking too much at what it offers from one side, as a certain experience obtained in prayer and faith. There is another side which God's Word puts very strongly, that of obedience as the only path to blessing. What we need to realize is that in our relationship to God He is the Infinite Being Who created and redeemed us. The first sentiment that ought to motivate us is that of subjection ,surrender to His supremacy, His glory, His will, and His pleasure.This ought to be the first and uppermost thought of our lives.

The question is not, however, how we are to obtain and enjoy His favor, for in this the main thing may still be self. What this Being in the very nature of things rightfully claims, and is infinitely and unspeakably worthy of, is that His glory and pleasure should be my only object. Surrender to His perfect and blessed will-a life of service and obedience-is the beauty and the charm of heaven. Service and obedience were the thoughts that were uppermost in the mind of the Son when He was on earth. Service and obedience must become the chief objects of our desires and aims, even more so than rest, light, joy, or strength.In them we will find the path to all the higher blessedness that awaits us.

Note what a prominent place the Master gives it, not only in this fifteenth chapter, in connection with the abiding, but in the fourteenth, where He speaks of the indwelling of the Trinity. John 14:15 says: "If ye love me, keep my commandments," and the Spirit will be given to you by the Father. Then verse 21:"He that hath my commandments and keepeth them,he it is that loveth me." He will have the special love of the Father and the special manifestation of Christ. Verse 23 is one of the highest of all the great and precious promises: "If a man loves me he will keep my words, and the Father and I will come and take up our abode with him." Could words put it more clearly that obedience is the way to the indwelling of the Spirit, to His revealing the Son within us, and to His preparing us to be the abode, the home of the Father? The indwelling of the Trinity is the heritage of those who obey.

Obedience and faith are simply two parts of one act-surrender to God and His will. As faith strengthens itself in order to be obedient, it is in turn strengthened by obedience. Faith is made perfect by works. Often our efforts to believe are unsuccessful because we don't assume the only position in which a large faith is legitimate or possible-that of entire surrender to the honor and the will of God. The man who is entirely consecrated to God and His will finds the power to claim everything that His God has promised to be for him.

The application of this in the school of prayer is very simple but very solemn. "I chose you, " the Master says, "and appointed you that ye should go and bear fruit, " much fruit (verses 5,8), "and that your fruit should abide, "that your life might be one of abiding fruit and abiding fruitfulness, "that" as fruitful branches abiding in me, "whatsoever ye shall ask of the Father in my name, He may give it you. "

How often we've tried to pray an effective prayer for grace to bear fruit and have wondered why the answer didn't come. It was because we were reversing the Master's order. We wanted to have the comfort, the joy, and the strength first, so we could do the work easily and without any feeling of difficulty or self-sacrifice. But He wanted us to do what He said in the obedience of faith, without worrying about whether we felt weak or strong, or whether the work was hard or easy. The path of fruit-bearing leads us to the place and the power of successful prayer.

Obedience is the only path that leads to the glory of God. Obedience doesn't replace faith or supply its shortcomings. But faith's obedience gives access to all the blessings our God has for us. In the Gospel of John, the baptism of the Spirit (John 14:16), the manifestation of the Son (14:21), the indwelling of the Father (14:23), the abiding in Christ's love (15:10), the privilege of His holy friendship (15:14), and the power of effective prayer (15:16), all wait for the obedient.

Now we know the great reason why we have not had power in faith to pray successfully. Our lives weren't as they should have been. Simple obedience-abiding fruitfulness-was not its chief mark. We whole-heartedly approve of the Divine appointment of men to whom God gives the power to rule the world. At their request, He does what otherwise would not have taken place. Their will guides the path in which God's will is to work. These men must have learned obedience themselves. Their loyalty and submission to authority must be above all suspicion. If we approve the law, that obedience and fruit-bearing are the path to prevailing prayer, we must with shame acknowledge how little our lives have exemplified this.

Let us yield ourselves to take up the appointment the Savior gives us. If we concentrate on our relationship to Him as our Master, we should no longer begin each new day with thoughts of comfort, joy, or blessing. Our first thought should be: "I belong to the Master." Every moment I must act as His property, as a part of Himself, as one who only seeks to know and do His will. I am a servant, a slave of Jesus Christ. Let this be the spirit that animates me. If He says, "No longer do I call you servants, but I have called you friends," let us accept the place of friends, because, "Ye are my friends if ye do the things which I command you."

The one thing He commands us as His branches is to bear fruit. Live to bless others, to testify of the life and the love there is in Jesus. In faith and obedience give your whole life to that which Jesus chose us for and appointed us to-fruitbearing. Think of His electing us to this, accepting your appointment as coming from Him Who always gives us everything He demands of us. We will grow strong in the confidence that a life of fruit-bearing and abiding is within our reach. And we will understand why this fruit-bearing alone can be the path to the place of all effective prayer. The man who, in obedience to Christ, proves that he is doing what his Lord wills, will receive whatever he desires from the Father. "Whatsoever we ask we receive, because we keep His commandments, and do the things that are pleasing in His sight."

Lord, teach us to pray.

Blessed Master! Teach me to understand fully what I only partly realize, that only by obeying the will of God can we obtain His promises and use them effectively in our prayers. Show me how bearing fruit perfects the deeper growth of the branch into the Vine, allowing us to experience that perfect union with- God in which we can ask for whatever we want.

O Lord! Reveal to us how with all the hosts of heaven, with all the saints here on earth, and even with Yourself on earth, that obedience to God is the highest privilege. It gives access to oneness with the Father Himself in that which is His highest glory-His all-perfect will. And show us how, if we keep Your commandments and bear fruit according to Your will, our spiritual natures will grow to the full stature of a perfect man, having power to ask and receive anything.

O Lord Jesus! Reveal Yourself to us! Through Your purpose and power, make Your wonderful promises the daily experience of everyone who completely yields himself to You and Your words. Amen.

CHAPTER 24:
THE ALL-POWERFUL PLEA

"And whatsoever ye shall ask in my name, that will I do ....If ye shall ask anything in my name, I will do it....that whatsoever ye shall ask of the Father in my name, he may give it to you .... Verily, verily, I say unto you, Whatsoever ye shall ask the Father in my name, he will give it to you .... Hitherto have ye asked nothing in my name: ask, and ye shall receive ....At that day ye shall ask in my name" (John 14:13-14;15:16; 16:23-24,26).

Until now the disciples had not asked in the Name of Christ, nor had He Himself ever used the expression. Here in His parting words, He repeats the word unceasingly in connection with those promises of unlimited meaning: "Whatsoever," "Anything," "What ye will. "He wanted to teach them and us that His Name is our only, but also our completely sufficient, plea. The power of prayer and its answer depend on the right use of the Name.

What is a person's name? It is a word or expression in which a person is represented to us. When I mention,or hear a name,it brings to mind the whole man, what I know of him, and also the impression he has made on me. The name of a king includes his honor, his power, and his kingdom. His name is the symbol of his power. And so each name of God embodies and represents some part of the glory of the Unseen One. The Name of Christ is the expression of everything He has done and everything He is and lives to do as our Mediator.

What does it mean to do a thing in the name of another? It is to come with his power and authority, as his representative and substitute. Using another's name always presupposes a common interest. No one would give another the free use of his name without first being assured that his honor and interests were as safe with that other person as with himself.

What does it mean when Jesus gives us power over His Name-the free use of it-with the assurance that whatever we ask in it will be given to us? The ordinary comparison of one person giving another, on some special occasion, the liberty to ask something in his name, comes altogether short here. Jesus solemnly gives to all His disciples a general and unlimited power to use His Name at all times for everything they desire. He could not do this if He did not know that He could trust us with His interests and that His honor would be safe in our hands.

The free use of someone else's name is always a token of great confidence and close union. Someone who gives his name to another stands aside to let that person act for him. Someone who takes the name of another gives up his own as of no value. When I go in the name of another, I deny myself. I take not only his name, but himself and what he is, instead of myself and what I am.

Such use of a person's name may be the result of a legal union. A merchant leaving his home and business gives his chief clerk a general power by which he can withdraw thousands of dollars in the merchant's name. The clerk does this, not for himself, but only in the interests of the business. Because the merchant knows and trusts him as wholly devoted to his interests and business, he dares put his name and property at his command.

When the Lord Jesus went to heaven, He left His work-the management of His Kingdom on earth in the hands of His servants. He also gave them His Name to draw all the supplies they needed for the due conduct of His business. Christ's servants have the spiritual power to use the Name of Jesus only insofar as they yield themselves to live only for the interests and the work of the Master. The use of the Name always supposes the surrender of our interests to Him Whom we represent.

Another use of a name may be because of a life union.(In the case of the merchant and his clerk, the union is temporary.) Oneness of life on earth gives oneness of name: A child has the father's name because he has his life. Often the child of a good father is honored or helped by others for the sake of the name he bears. But this would not last long if it were found that it was only a name, and that the father's character wasn't present in it. The name and the character or spirit must be in harmony. When such is the case, the child will have a double claim on the father's friends. The character secures and increases the love and esteem extended at first for the name's sake.

It is the same with Jesus and the believer: We are one; we have one life and one Spirit with Him. For this reason we may proceed in His Name. Our power in using that Name, whether with God, men, or devils, depends on the measure of our spiritual life union with Christ. Our use of His Name rests on the unity of our lives with Him.

The Name and the Spirit of Jesus are one. "Whatsoever ye shall ask in my Name" means "in my nature." With God, things are requested according to their nature. Asking in Christ's Name doesn't mean that at the end of some request we say, "This I ask in the Name of Jesus Christ." It means we are praying according to His nature, which is love that doesn't seek its own will, but only the will of God and the good of all creatures. Such asking is the cry of Christ's own Spirit in our hearts.

The union that gives power to the use of the Name may be the union of love. When a bride whose life has been one of poverty becomes united to the bridegroom, she gives up her own name to be called by his, and has the full right to use it. She purchases in his name, and that name is not refused. This is done because the bridegroom has chosen her for himself, counting on her to care for his interests because they are now one.

The heavenly Bridegroom does nothing less. Having loved

us and made us one with Himself, what can He do but give those who bear His Name the right to present it before the Father, or to come with it to Himself for all they need? No one really gives himself up to live in the Name of Jesus without receiving in ever-increasing measure the spiritual capacity to ask for and receive in that Name whatever he desires. My bearing of the name of another shows that I have given up my own name and, with it, my own independent life. But just as surely, it shows I have possession of everything belonging to the name I have taken instead of my own.

The common comparison to a messenger sent to ask in the name of another, or a guilty person using the name of a guardian in his appeal, is defective. We are not praying in the name of someone who is absent. Jesus Himself is with the Father. When we pray to the Father, it must be in Jesus' Name. The Name represents the person. To ask in His Name is to ask in full union of interest, life, and love with Himself, as one who lives in and for Him.

Let the Name of Jesus have undivided supremacy in my heart and life! My faith will grow to the assurance that what I ask for in that Name cannot be refused. The Name and the power of asking go together. When the Name of Jesus has become the power that rules my life, its power in prayer with God will be seen, too.

Everything depends on my own relationship to the Name. The power it has on my life is the power it will have in my prayers. There is more than one expression in Scripture which can make this clear. "Do all in the Name of the Lord Jesus" is the counterpart of "Ask all. " To do all and ask all in His Name go together. "We shall walk in the Name of our God" means the power of the Name must rule in the whole life. Only then will it have power in prayer. God looks not to our lips, but to our lives to see what the Name is to us. When Scripture speaks of "men who have given their lives for the Name of the Lord Jesus," or of one "ready to die for the Name of the Lord Jesus," we see what our relationship to the Name must be. When it is everything to me, it will obtain everything for me. If I let it have all I have, it will let me have all it has.

" Whatsoever ye shall ask in my Name, that will I do." Jesus means that promise literally. Christians have sought to limit it because it looked too free. It was hardly safe to trust man so unconditionally. They did not understand that the phrase "in my Name" is its own safeguard. It is a spiritual power which no one can use further than his living and acting in that Name allows.

As we bear the Name before men, we have the power to use it before God. Let us plead for God's Holy Spirit to show us what the Name means, and what the right use of it is. It is through the Spirit that the Name, which is above every name in heaven, will take the place of supremacy in our hearts and lives, too. Disciples of Jesus! Let the lessons of this day go deeply into your hearts. The Master says, "Only pray in my Name; whatsoever ye ask will be given. Heaven is opened to you! The treasures and power of the spiritual world are placed at your disposal to help those around you.

Learn to pray in the Name of Jesus. He says to us as He said to the disciples, "Hitherto ye have not asked in my Name: ask, and ye shall receive." Let each disciple of Jesus seek to avail himself of the rights of his royal priesthood, to use the power placed at his disposal for his work. Let Christian awake and hear this message: Your prayers can obtain what would otherwise be withheld! They can accomplish what would otherwise remain undone O awake, and use the Name of Jesus to open the treasures of heaven for this perishing world!

Lord, teach us to pray!

Blessed Lord! It seems as if each lesson You give me has such depth of meaning that if I could just learn that one, I would be able to pray properly. Right now I feel as if I only need to pray for one thing: Lord, please teach me what it is to pray inYour Name. Teach me to live and act, to walk and speak, to do everything in the Name of Jesus, so that my prayer cannot be anything else but in that blessed Name, too.

Lord! Teach me to fully grasp the precious promise that whatever I ask in Your name You will do. and the Father will give. I realize that I haven't fully attained, and that I don't completely understand, the wondrous union You mean when You say, "In my Name." Let me hold on to the promise until it fills my heart with the undoubting assurance that I can ask for anything in the Name of Jesus.

O my Lord! Let the Holy Spirit teach me this! You did describe Him as "the Comforter, Whom the Father shall send in My Name. "He knows what it is to be sent from heaven in Your Name, to reveal and to honor the power of that Name in Your servants; and to use that Name alone to glorify You. Lord Jesus! Let Your Spirit dwell in me and fill me! I yield my whole being to His rule and leading. Your Name and Your Spirit are one. Through Him, Your Name will be the strength of my life and my prayer. Then I will be able to forsake everything for Your Name's sake, speaking to men and to God in Your Name, and proving that this, indeed, is the Name above every name.

Lord Jesus! Please teach me by Your Holy Spirit to pray in Your Name. Amen.

CHAPTER 25:
THE HOLY SPIRIT AND PRAYER

"And in that day ye shall ask me nothing. Verily, verily, I say unto you, Whatsoever ye shall ask the Farther in my name, he will give it you. Hitherto have ye asked nothing in my name: ask, and ye shall receive, that your joy may be full" (John 16:23-24).

"At that day ye shall ask in my name: and I say not unto you, that I will pray the Father for you: For the Father himself loveth you" (John 16:26-27).

"Praying in the Holy Ghost, keep yourselves in the love of God" (Jude 20-21).

The words of John (I John 2:12-14) to little children, young men, and fathers suggest the thought that often in the Christian life there are three great stages of experience. The first, that of the new-born child, is filled with the assurance and the joy of forgiveness. The second, the transition stage of struggle and growth in knowledge and strength, is comparable to young men growing strong. God's Word is doing its work in them and giving them victory over the evil one. The final stage of maturity and ripeness is that of the fathers, who have entered deeply into the knowledge and fellowship of the Eternal One.

In Christ's teaching on prayer, three similar stages in prayerlife are apparent. The Sermon on the Mount describes the initial stage. All of His teaching is comprised in one word: Father. Pray to your Father; your Father sees, hears, knows, and will reward. How much more than any earthly father He is! Simply be childlike and trustful.

Then comes something like a transition stage of conflict and conquest. Words like these refer to it: "This sort goeth not out but by prayer and fasting""Shall not God avenge His own elect who cry day and night unto Him?"

Finally, we have in the parting words a higher stage: The children have become men. They are now the Master's friends, from whom He has no secrets, and to whom He says, "All things that I heard from my Father I made known unto you." In the frequently repeated "whatsoever ye will," He hands them the keys of the Kingdom. Now the time has come for the power of prayer in His Name to be proved.

The contrast between this final stage and the previous preparatory ones is marked most distinctly in the words: "Hitherto ye have asked nothing in my Name"; "At that day ye shall ask in my Name." "At that day" means the day of the outpouring of the Holy Spirit. The great work Christ was to do on the cross-the mighty power and the complete victory to be manifested in His resurrection and ascension would allow the glory of God to come down from heaven as never before, to dwell in men. The Spirit of the glorified Jesus was to come and be the life of His disciples. And one of the signs of that wonderful, new flow of the Spirit was to be a power in prayer that was up to that time unknown. Prayer in the Name of Jesus-asking for and obtaining everything-is to be the evidence of the reality of the Spirit's indwelling.

The coming of the Holy Spirit indeed began a new epoch in the prayer world. To understand this, we must remember Who He is, what His work is, and why His not being given until Jesus was glorified is significant. It is in the Spirit that God exists, for He is Spirit. It is in the Spirit that the Son was begotten of the Father, because in the fellowship of the Spirit, the Father and the Son are one. The Father's prerogative is eternal, continuous giving to the Son. The Son's right and blessedness is to ask and receive eternally. Through the Spirit, this communion of life and love is maintained. This has been true from all eternity.

It is especially true now, when the Son as Mediator lives to pray. The great work which Jesus began on earth of reconciling God and man in His own body, He carries on in heaven. To accomplish this, He took the conflict between God's righteousness and our sin into His own person. On the cross, He ended the struggle once and for all in His own body. Then He ascended to heaven, where He carries out the deliverance He obtained and manifests His victory in each member of His Body. This is why He lives to pray. In His unceasing intercession, He places Himself in living fellowship with the unceasing prayer of His redeemed ones. Or rather, it is His unceasing intercession which shows itself in their prayers, giving them a power they never had before.

He does this through the Holy Spirit. This Spirit of the glorified Jesus was not manifested and could not be until Jesus had been glorified (John 7:39). This gift of the Father was something distinctively new, entirely different from what the Old Testament saints had known. The work that the blood effected in heaven when Christ entered within the veil was totally true and new. The redemption of human nature into fellowship with His resurrection power and His glory was intensely real. The taking up of our humanity through Christ into the life of the triune God was an event of such inconceivable significance, that the Holy Spirit was indeed no longer only what He had been in the Old Testament.

That "the Holy Spirit was not yet, for Christ was not yet glorified" was literally true. The Holy Spirit had come from Christ's exalted humanity to testify in our hearts of what Christ had accomplished. Just as Jesus, after having come to earth as a man, returned to heaven with power He didn't have before, so the Holy Spirit came to us with a new life which He hadn't had before. He came to us with that new life-as the Spirit of the glorified Jesus. Under the Old Testament He was invoked as the Spirit of God.At Pentecost He descended as the Spirit of the glorified Jesus, bringing down and communicating to us the full fruit and power of the accomplished redemption.

Christ's continuing intercession maintains the effectiveness and application of His redemption. The Holy Spirit descending from Christ to us draws us up into the great stream of His ascending prayers. The Spirit prays for us without words in the depths of a heart where even thoughts are at times formless. He takes us up into the wonderful flow of the life of the triune God. Through the Spirit, Christ's prayers become ours, and ours are made His. We ask for what we desire, and it is given to us. We then understand from experience, "Hitherto ye have not asked in my Name. At that day ye shall ask in my Name."

Brother! What we need in order to pray in the Name of Christ to ask that we may receive that our joy may be full-is the baptism of this Holy Spirit. This is more than the Spirit of God under the Old Testament. This is more than the Spirit of conversion and regeneration the disciples had before Pentecost. This is more than the Spirit with a portion of Christ's influence and power. This is the Holy Spirit, the Spirit of the glorified Jesus in His exaltation and power, coming to us as the Spirit of the indwelling Jesus, revealing the Son and the Father within us (John 14:16-23). This Spirit cannot simply be the Spirit of our hours of prayer. It must be the Spirit of our whole life and walk, glorifying Jesus in us by revealing the completeness of His work and making us wholly one with Him and like Him. Then we can pray in His Name, because we are in very deed one with Him. Then we have that immediate access to the Father of which Jesus says, "I say not unto you, that I will pray the Father for you" (John 16:26).

Oh! We need to understand and believe that to be filled with the Spirit of the Glorified One is the one need of God's believing people. Then we will be able "with all prayer and supplication to be praying at all seasons in the Spirit," and "praying in the Holy Ghost, to keep ourselves in the love of God." "At that day ye shall ask in my Name."

Once again, we learn this lesson: What our prayer achieves depends on what we are and what our lives are. Living in the Name of Christ is the secret of praying in the Name of Christ; living in the Spirit is necessary for praying in the Spirit. Abiding in Christ gives the right and power to ask for what we desire. The extent of our abiding is equivalent to our power in prayer. The Spirit dwelling within us prays, not always in words and thoughts, but in a breathing and a being that is deeper than utterance. There is as much real prayer in us as there is of Christ's Spirit. Let our lives be full of Christ and full of His Spirit, so that the wonderfully unlimited promises to our prayers will no longer appear strange. "Hitherto ye have asked nothing in my Name. Ask, and ye shall receive, that your joy may be full. At that day ye shall ask in my Name. Verily, verily, I say unto you, Whatsoever ye shall ask the Father in my Name, He will give it you."

Lord, teach us to pray.

O my God! In holy awe I bow before You, the Three in One. Again I see how the mystery of prayer is the mystery of the Holy Trinity. I adore the Father Who always hears. I adore the Son Who lives eternally to pray. And I love the Holy Spirit Who comes from the Father and the Son, lifting us up into the fellowship of that blessed, never-ceasing asking and receiving. I bow, my God, in adoring worship before the infinite power which, through the Holy Spirit, takes us and our prayers into Your Divine life and its fellowship of love.

O my blessed Lord Jesus! Teach me to understand this lesson: The indwelling Spirit streaming from You and uniting us to You is the Spirit of prayer. Teach me how, as an empty, wholly consecrated vessel, to yield myself to His being my life. Teach me to honor Him and to trust Him, as a living Person, to lead my life and my prayer. Teach me especially in prayer to wait in holy silence, giving Him time to breathe His unutterable intercession within me. And teach me that through Him it is possible to pray without ceasing and to pray without failing, because He makes me a partaker of the never-ceasing and never-failing intercession in which You appear before the Father.

O Lord! Fulfill in me Your promise, "At that day ye shall ask in my Name. Verily, verily, I say unto you, Whatsoever ye shall ask the Father in my Name, that will He give." Amen.

AUTHOR'S NOTE

Prayer has often been compared to breathing. We have to carry out the comparison fully to see how wonderful the place is which the Holy Spirit occupies. With every breath, we expel impure air which would soon cause our death, and inhale fresh air to which we owe our life. In confession we release our sins, and in prayer we release the needs and desires of our hearts. And we inhale the fresh air of the promises, the love, and the life of God in Christ. We do this through the Holy Spirit, Who is the breath of our life.

He is also the breath of God. The Father breathes Him into us to unite Himself with our life. Just as every expiration is followed by the inhaling of the next breath, so God inhales His breath, and the Spirit returns to Him laden with the desires and needs of our hearts.

Thus the Holy Spirit is the breath of the life of God and the breath of the new life in us. As God breathes Him out, we receive Him in answer to prayer: as we breathe Him back again, He rises to God carrying our petitions. It is though the Holy Spirit that the Father and the Son are one, and that the intercession of the Son reaches the Father. He is our Spirit of prayer. True prayer is the living experience of the truth of the Holy Trinity. The Spirit's breathing, the Son's intercession, and the Father's will become one in us.

CHAPTER 26:
CHRIST THE INTERCESSOR

"But I have prayed for thee, that thy faith fail not" (Luke 22:32).

"I say not unto you, that I will pray the Father for you" (John 16:26).

"He ever liveth to make intercession for them" (Hebrews 7:25).

All growth in the spiritual life is connected with clearer insight into what Jesus is to us. The more I realize that Christ must be everything to me and in me, that everything in Christ is indeed for me, the more I learn to live the real life of faith. This life dies to self and lives wholly in Christ. The Christian life is no longer a vain struggle to live right, but a resting in Christ to find strength in Him as life. He helps us fight and gain the victory of faith!

This is especially true of the life of prayer. It, too, comes under the law of faith alone, and is seen in the light of the fullness and completeness there is in Jesus. The believer understands that prayer is no longer a matter of strain or anxious care, but an experience of what Christ will do for him and in him. It is a participation in the life of Christ, which is the same on earth as in heaven, always ascending to the Father as prayer. So he begins to pray. Such a believer not only trusts the merits of Jesus, or His intercession, by which our unworthy prayers are made acceptable: He also trusts in that near and close union through which He prays in us and we in Him. Having Him within us, we abide in Him and He in us through the Holy Spirit perfecting our union with Him, so that we ourselves can come directly to the Father in His Name.

The whole of salvation is Christ Himself: He has given Himself to us. He Himself lives in us. Because He prays, we pray, too. Just like the disciples, when they saw Jesus praying and asked Him to make them partakers of what He knew of prayer, we know that He makes us participate with Himself in the life of prayer. He is now our Intercessor on the throne.

This comes out quite clearly in the last night of His life. In His high-priestly prayer (John 17), He shows us how and what He has to pray to the Father, and what He will pray when He ascends to heaven. He had in His parting address repeatedly connected His going to the Father with their new life of prayer. The two would be ultimately connected. His entrance on the work of His eternal intercession would be the commencement and the power of their new prayer-life in His Name. It is the sight of Jesus in His intercession that gives us power to pray in His Name. All right and power of prayer is Christ's; He makes us share in His intercession.

To understand this, think first of His intercession. He lives to intercede. The work of Christ on earth as Priest was just a beginning. As Aaron, who offered the blood sacrifice, Jesus shed His blood. As Melchizedek, He now lives within the veil to continue His work for the power of the eternal life.

"It is Christ that died: yea rather, who is even at the right hand of God, who maketh intercession for us." That intercession is an intense reality-a work that is absolutely necessary-and without which the continued application of redemption cannot take place. Through the incarnation and resurrection of Jesus, the wondrous reconciliation took place, and man became partaker of the Divine life and blessedness.

But the real, personal use of this reconciliation cannot take place without the unceasing exercise of His Divine power by the Head in heaven. In all conversion and sanctification, in every victory over sin and the world, there is a real exercise of Christ's power. This exercise takes place only through His prayer: He asks of the Father and receives from the Father. "He is able to save them to the uttermost because He ever liveth to make intercession" (Hebrews 7:25). He receives every need of His people in intercession, extending to them what the Godhead has to give. His mediation on the throne is as real and indispensable as it was on the cross. Nothing takes place without Christ's intercession. It engages all His time and all His power. It is His unceasing occupation at the right hand of the Father.

We participate, not only in the benefits of HIS work, but in the work itself. This is because we are His Body. The Head and the members are one: "The head cannot say to the feet, I have no need of thee" (I Corinthians 12:21). We share with Jesus everything He is and has. "The glory which Thou gavest me, I have given them" (John 17:22). We are partakers of His life, His righteousness, and His work. We share His intercession, too. He cannot do it without us.

"Christ is our life"; "No longer I, but Christ liveth in me." The life in Him and in us is identical; it is one and the same. His life in heaven is a life of continuous prayer. When it descends and takes possession of us, it does not lose its character. It becomes a life of continuous prayer in us, too. It is a life that without ceasing asks and receives from God.

This is not as if there were two separate currents of prayer rising upwards-one from Him and one from His people. A substantial life-union is also a prayer-union. What He prays passes though us, and what we pray passes through Him. He is the angel with the golden censer. "Unto Him there was given much incense"-the secret of acceptable prayer -"that He should offer it with the prayers of all the saints upon the golden altar" (Revelation 8:3). We live and abide in Him, the Interceding One.

The Only-begotten is the only One Who has the right to pray. To Him alone it was said, "Ask, and it shall be given Thee." Just as the fullness for all things dwells in Him, a true fullness in prayer dwells in Him, too. He alone has the power of prayer. Growth of the spiritual life consists of a deeper belief that all treasures are in Him, and that we, too, are in Him. We receive each moment what we possess in Him. Prayer-life is the same. Our faith in the intercession of Jesus must not only be in His praying for us when we do not or cannot pray. As the Author of our life and our faith, He draws us to pray in unison with Himself. Our prayer must be a work of faith in the sense that as we know that Jesus communicates His whole life in us, He also breathes our praying into us.

To many a believer, it was a new epoch in his spiritual life when it was revealed to him how truly and entirely Christ was his life, standing responsible for his remaining faithful and obedient. It was then, that he really began to live a life of faith. No less blessed will be the discovery that Christ is responsible for our prayer-life, too. As the center and embodiment of all prayer, it is communicated by Him through the Holy Spirit to His people.

"He ever liveth to make intercession" as the Head of the Body. He is the Leader in that new and living way which He has opened up as the Author and the Perfecter of our faith. He provides everything for the life of His redeemed ones by giving His own life in them. He cares for their life of prayer by taking them up into His heavenly prayer-life, giving and maintaining His prayer-life within them. "I have prayed for thee," not to render thy faith needless, but "that thy faith fail not." Our faith and prayer of faith is rooted in His. If we pray with and in the eternal Intercessor, abiding in Him, "ask whatsoever ye will, and it shall be done unto you."

The thought of our fellowship in the intercession of Jesus reminds us of what He has taught us more than once before. All these wonderful prayer-promises have the glory of God, in the manifestation of His Kingdom and the salvation of sinners, as their aim. As long as we pray chiefly for ourselves, the promises of the last night must remain a sealed book to us. The promises are given to the fruit-bearing branches of the Vine, to disciples sent into the world to live for perishing men as the Father sent Him, to His faithful servants and intimate friends who take up the work He leaves behind. Like their Lord, they have become seed-corn, losing their lives to multiply them.

Let us each find out what our work is, and which souls are entrusted to our special prayers. Let us make our intercession for them our life of fellowship with God. We will not only discover the truth to the promises of power in prayer. We will begin to realize how our abiding in Christ and His abiding in us makes us share in His own joy of blessing and saving men.

O most wonderful intercession of our Blessed Lord Jesus! We not only owe everything to that intercession, but in it we are taken up as active partners and fellow-workers! Now we understand what it is to pray in the Name of Jesus, and why it has such power. To pray in His Name, in His Spirit, in Himself, and in perfect union with Him is the active and effective intercession of Christ Jesus. When will we ever be wholly taken up into it?

Lord, teach us to pray!

Blessed Lord! In lowly adoration I again bow before You. All of Your work of redemption has now passed into prayer. You are completely occupied with praying, to maintain and dispense what You purchased with Your blood. You live to pray. And because we abide in You, we have direct access to the Father. Our lives can be lives of unceasing prayer, and the answer to our prayer is certain.

Blessed Lord! You have invited Your people to be Your fellow-workers in a life of prayer. You have united Yourself with Your people. As Your Body, they share the ministry of intercession with You. Only through this ministry can the world be filled with the fruit of Your redemption and the glory of the Father. With more liberty than ever I come to You, my Lord, and plead with You to teach me to pray. Your life is prayer; Your life is mine. Lord! Teach me to pray in You and like You.

And, O my Lord! Let me know, just as You promised Your disciples, that You are in the Father, I am in You, and You are in me. Let the uniting power of the Holy Spirit make my whole life an abiding in You and in Your intercession. May my prayer be its echo, so that the Father hears me in You and You in me. Lord Jesus! In everything, let Your mind be in me! In everything, let my life be in Y ou! In this way, I will be prepared to be the channel, Through which Your intercession pours its blessing on the world. Amen.

CHAPTER 27:
CHRIST THE HIGH PRIEST

"Father, I will that they also, whom thou hast given me, be with me where I am '(John 17:24).

In His parting address, Jesus gives His disciples the full revelation of what the new life was to be when the Kingdom of God had come in power. They were to find their calling and their blessedness in the indwelling of the Holy Spirit, in union with Jesus, the heavenly Vine, and in their witnessing and suffering for Him. As He described their future life, the Lord had repeatedly given the most unlimited promises as to the power their prayers might have.

Now in closing, He Himself proceeds to pray. To let His disciples have the joy Of knowing what His intercession for them in heaven as their High Priest will be, He gives them this precious legacy of His prayer to the Father. He does this because, as priests, they are to share in His work of intercession, and they must know how to perform this holy work.

In the teaching of our Lord on this last night (John, chapter

17), we recognize that these astonishing prayer-promises have not been given for our benefit, but in the interest of the Lord and His Kingdom. Only from the Lord Himself can we learn what prayer in His Name is to be and what it can obtain. To pray in His Name is to pray in perfect unity with Himself. The High-Priestly prayer will teach everyone that prayer in the Name of Jesus may ask for and expect everything. This prayer is ordinarily divided into three parts. Our Lord first prays for Himself (verses 1-5), then for His disciples (verses 6-19), and last for all the believing people of all ages (verses 20-26). The follower of Jesus who gives himself to the work of intercession, and who would like to know how much of a blessing he can pray down upon his circle in the Name of Jesus, should in all humility let himself be led of the Spirit to study this wonderful prayer as one of the most important lessons of the school of prayer.

First of all, Jesus prays for Himself, for His being glorified, so that He may glorify the Father. "Father! Glorify Thy Son. And now, Father, glorify Me." He presents reasons for His praying this way. A holy convenant was concluded between the Father and the Son in heaven. The Father promised Him power over all flesh as the reward for His work. Now Jesus had done the work, He had glorified the Father, and His one purpose was to further glorify Him. With the utmost boldness He asks the Father to glorify Him, so that He may now be and do for His people everything He has undertaken.

Disciple of Jesus! Here you have the first lesson in your work of priestly intercession, to be learned from the example of your great High Priest. To pray in the Name of Jesus is to pray in unity and in sympathy with Him. The Son began His prayer by clarifying His relationship to the Father, speaking of His work and obedience and His desire to see the Father glorified. You should pray like this. Draw near to the Father in Christ. Plead His finished work. Say that you are one with it, that you trust it, and live in it. Say that you, too, have given yourself to finish the work the Father has given you to do, and to live alone for His glory. Then ask confidently that the Son may be glorified in you.

This is praying in the Name, in the very words, and in the Spirit of Jesus, in union with Jesus Himself. Such prayer has power. If with Jesus you glorify the Father, the Father will glorify Jesus by doing what you ask in His Name. It is only when your own personal relationship, like Christ's, is clear with God-when you are glorifying Him and seeking everything for His glory-that, like Christ, you will have power to intercede for those around you.

Our Lord next prays for the circle of His disciples. He speaks of them as those whom the Father has given Him. Their distinguishing characteristic is that they have received Christ's Word. He says He is now sending them into the world in His place, just as the Father had sent Him. He asks two things for them: that the Father would keep them from the evil one, and that He would sanctify them through His Word.

Just like the Lord, each believing intercessor has his own immediate circle for whom he prays first. Parents have their children, teachers their pupils, pastors their flocks, and all believers have those whose care lies on their hearts. It is of great consequence that intercession should be personal, pointed, and definite. Our first prayer must always be that they receive the Word.

But this prayer will not work unless we say to the Lord, "I have given them Your Word." This gives us liberty and power in intercession for souls. Don't just pray for them, but speak to them. When they have received the Word, pray for their being kept from the evil one and for their being sanctified through that Word. Instead of being hopeless or judging, or giving up on those who fall, let us pray, "Father! Keep them in Your Name! Sanctify them through Your truth!" Prayer in the Name of Jesus accomplishes much: "What ye will shall be done unto you."

Next our Lord prays for a still wider circle. "I pray not only for these, but for them who through their word shall believe." His priestly heart enlarges itself to embrace all places and all time. He prays that everyone who belongs to Him may everywhere be one, as God's proof to the world of the divinity of His mission. He then prays that they may always be with Him in His glory. Until then, He asks "that the love wherewith Thou last loved me may be in them, and I in them."

The disciple of Jesus who has first proved the power of prayer in his own circle cannot confine himself within its limits. He then prays for the universal Church and its different branches. He prays especially for the unity of the Spirit and of love. He prays for its being one in Christ, as a witness to the world that Christ, Who has made love triumph over selfishness and separation, is indeed the Son of God sent from heaven. Every believer ought to pray that the unity of the Church, not in external organizations, but in spirit and in truth, is manifested.

Jesus says, "Father! I will (or I desire)." Based on His right as Son, the Father's promise to Him, and His finished work, He can do so. The Father had said to Him, "Ask of me, and I will give Thee." He simply availed Himself of the Father's promise. Jesus has given us a similar promise: "Whatsoever ye will shall be done unto you." He asks me in His Name to say what I will, what I desire. Abiding in Him, in a living union with Him in which man is nothing and Christ is everything, the believer has the liberty to take up that word of His High Priest. In answer to the question, "What wilt thou? "to say, "Father! I will all that You have promised."

This is nothing but true faith. It honors God that I have such confidence in saying what I desire is indeed acceptable to Him. At first sight, our hearts shrink from the expression. We feel neither the liberty nor the power to speak in such a manner. But grace will most assuredly be given to each one who loses his will in his Lord's. Whoever gives up his will entirely will find it again renewed and strengthened with a Divine strength.

"Father! I will. " This is the keynote of the everlasting, ever-active, all-powerful intercession of our Lord in heaven. It is only in union with Him that our prayer is effective and accomplishes much. If we abide in Him, living, walking, and doing all things in His Name; if we take each separate petition, tested and touched by His Word and Spirit, and cast it into the mighty stream of intercession that goes up from Him to be presented before the Father; then we will have the full confidence that we receive what we ask for. The cry "Father! I will "will be breathed into us by the Spirit Himself. We will lose ourselves in Him and become nothing, finding that in our impotence we have power to succeed.

Disciples of Jesus! You are called to be like your Lord in His priestly intercession! When will we awaken to the glory of our destiny to pray to God for perishing men and be answered? When will we shake off the sloth that clothes itself in the pretense of humility and yield ourselves wholly to God's Spirit, that He might fill our wills with light and power to know, to take, and to possess everything that our God is waiting to give?

Lord, teach us to pray.

O my Blessed High Priest! Who am I that You should invite me to share Your power of intercession? And why, O my Lord, am I so slow of heart to understand, believe, and exercise this wonderful privilege to which You have redeemed Your people? O Lord! Give me Your grace, that my life's work may become praying without ceasing, to draw down the blessing of heaven on all my surrroundings on earth.

Blessed Lord! I come now to accept my calling, for which I will give up everything and follow You. Into Your hands I will believingly yield my whole being. Form, train, and inspire me to be one of Your prayer force, those who watch and strive in prayer, who have power and victory. Take possession of my heart, and fill it with the desire to glorify God in the gathering, sanctification, and union of those whom the Father has given You. Take my mind and give me wisdom to know when prayer can bring a blessing. Take me wholly and prepare me as You would a priest, to stand always before God and to bless His Name.

Blessed Lord! Now and through all my spiritual life, let me want everything for You, and nothing for myself. Let it be my experience that the peson who has and asks for nothing for himself, receives everything, including the wonderful grace of sharing Your everlasting ministry of intercession. Amen.

CHAPTER 28:
CHRIST THE SACRIFICE

"And he said, Abba, Father, all things are possible unto thee; take away this cup from me: nevertheless, not what I will, but what thou wilt" (Mark 14:36).

What a contrast within the space of a few hours! What a transition from the quiet elevation of that, "He lifted up His eyes to heaven, and said, Father! I will," to that falling on the ground and crying in agony, "My Father! not what I will." In the one we see the High Priest within the veil in His all powerful intercession; in the other, the sacrifice on the altar opening the way through the rent veil. The High-Priestly "Father! I will" precedes the sacrificial "Father! not what I will," but this was only to show what the intercession would be once the sacrifice was brought. The prayer before the throne, "Father! I will," had its origin and its power in the prayer at the altar, "Father! not what I will." From the entire surrender of His will in Gethsemane, the High Priest on the throne has the power to ask what He will, and the right to make His people share that power, asking what they will.

For everyone who wants to learn to pray in the school of

Jesus, this Gethsemane lesson is one of the most sacred and precious. To a superficial scholar, it may appear to take away the courage to pray in faith. If even the earnest supplication of the Son was not heard, if even He had to say, "Not what I will!" how much more we must need to say it! Thus it appears impossible that the promises which the Lord had given only a few hours previously, "Whatsoever ye shall ask," "Whatsoever ye will," could have been meant literally.

A deeper insight into the meaning of Gethsemane would teach us the sure way to the assurance of an answer to our prayers. Gaze in reverent and adoring wonder on this great sight: God's Son praying through His tears, and not obtaining what He asks. He Himself is our Teacher and will open up to us the mystery of His holy sacrifice, as revealed in this wondrous prayer.

To understand the prayer, let us note the infinite difference between what our Lord prayed earlier as royal High Priest, and what He here prays in His weakness. There He prayed to glorify the Father and to glorify Himself and His people as the fulfillment of distinct promises that had been given to Him. He asked what He knew would be according to the Word and the will of the Father. He could boldly say, "Father! I will."

Here He prays for something in regard to which the Father's will is not yet clear to Him. As far as He knows, it is the Father's will that He should drink the cup. He had told His disciples of the cup He must drink. A little later He would again say, "The cup which my Father hath given me, shall I not drink it?" It was for this He had come to this earth. But in

222

the unutterable agony of soul that gripped Him as the power of darkness overcame Him, He began to taste the first drops of death-the wrath of God against sin. His human nature, as it shuddered in the presence of the awful reality of being made a curse, gave utterance in this cry of anguish. Its desire was that, if God's purpose could be accomplished without it, He might be spared the awful cup: "Let this cup pass from me." That desire was the evidence of the intense reality of His humanity.

The "Not as I will" kept that desire from being sinful. He pleadingly cries, "All things are possible with Thee," and returns again to still more earnest prayer that the cup may be removed. "Not what I will," repeated three times, constitutes the very essence and worth of His sacrifice. He had asked for something of which He could not say, "I know it is Thy will." He had pleaded God's power and love, and had then withdrawn his plea in His final, "Thy will be done." The prayer that the cup should pass away could not be answered. The prayer of submission that God's will be done was heard and gloriously answered in His victory first over the fear, and then over the power of death.

In this denial of His will, this complete surrender of His will to the will of the Father, Christ's obedience reached its highest perfection. From the sacrifice of the will in Gethsemane, the sacrifice of the life on Calvary derives its value. It is here, as Scripture says, that He learned obedience and became the Author of everlasting salvation to everyone who obeys Him. Because in that prayer He became obedient until death-the death of the cross-God exalted Him highly and gave Him the

223

power to ask what He will. It was in that"Father! not what I will," that He obtained the power for the "Father! I will." By Christ's submittal in Gethsemane, He secured for His people the right to say to them, "Ask whatsoever ye will."

Let us look at the deep mysteries that Gethsemane offers. First, the Father offers His Well-beloved the cup of wrath. Second, the Son, Who is always so obedient, shrinks back and implores that He may not have to drink it. Third, the Father does not grant the Son His request, but still gives the cup. And last, the Son yields His will, is content that His will be not done, and goes out to Calvary to drink the cup. O Gethsemane! In you I see how my Lord could give me such unlimited assurance of an answer to my prayers. He won it for me by His consent to have His petition unanswered.

This is in harmony with the whole scheme of redemption. Our Lord always wins for us the opposite of what He suffered. He was bound so that we could go free. He was made sin so that we could become the righteousness of God. He died so that we could live. He bore God's curse so that God's blessing would be ours. He endured God's not answering His prayer, so that our prayers could find an answer. He said, "Not as I will, "so that He could say to us, "If ye abide in me, ask what ye will, and it shall be done unto you."

"If ye abide in me": Here in Gethsemane the word acquires new force and depth. Christ is our Head, Who stands in our place and bears what we would otherwise have had to bear forever. We deserved that God should turn a deaf ear to us and never listen to our cries. Christ came and suffered for us.

He suffered what we had merited. For our sins, He suffered beneath the burden of that unanswered prayer. But now His suffering succeeds for me. What He has borne is taken away from me. His merit has won for me the answer to every prayer, if I abide in Him.

Yes, in Him, as He bows there in Gethsemane, I must abide. As my Head, He not only once suffered for me, but He always lives in me, breathing and working His own nature in me. The Spirit through which He offered Himself to God is the Spirit that dwells in me, too. He makes me a partaker of the very same obedience and the sacrifice of the will to God. That Spirit teaches me to yield my will entirely to the will of the Father, to give it up even unto death. He teaches me to distrust whatever is of my own mind, thought, and will, even though it may not be directly sinful. He opens my ear to wait in great gentleness and teachableness of soul for what the Father day by day has to speak and to teach. He shows me how union with God's will (and the love of it) is union with God Himself. Entire surrender to God's will is the Father's claim, the Son's example, and the true blessedness of the soul.

The Spirit leads my will into the fellowship of Christ's death and resurrection. My will dies in Him, and in Him is made alive again. He breathes into it a holy insight into God's perfect will, a holy joy in yielding itself to be an instrument of that will, and a holy liberty and power to lay hold of God's will to answer prayer. With my whole will, I learn to live for the interests of God and His Kingdom and to exercise the power of that will-crucified but risen again -in nature and in prayer, on earth and in heaven, with men and with God.

The more deeply I enter into the "Father! not what I will" of Gethsemane, and into Him Who said it, the fuller is my spiritual access to the power of His "Father! I will." The soul experiences that the will has become nothing in order that God's will may be everything. It is now inspired with a Divine strength to really will what God wills, and to claim what has been promised to it in the Name of Christ.

Listen to Christ in Gethsemane as He calls, "If ye abide in me, ye shall ask what ye will, and it shall be done unto you." Be of one mind and spirit with Him in His giving up everything to God's will; live like Him in obedience and surrender to the Father. This is abiding in Him-the secret of power in prayer.

Lord, teach us to pray

Blessed Lord Jesus! Gethsemane was the school where You learned to pray and to obey. It is still Your school, where You lead all Your disciples who wish to learn to obey and to pray just like You Lord! Teach me there to pray, in the faith that You have atoned for and conquered our self-will and can indeed give us grace to pray like you.

O Lamb of God! I want to follow You to Gethsemane! There I want to become one with You and abide in You, as You to the very death yield Your will to the Father. With You, through You, and in You, I yield my will in absolute and entire surrender to the will of the Father. Conscious of my own weakness and the secret power with which self-will would assert itself and again take its place on the throne, I claim in faith the power of Your victory. You have triumphed over it and delivered me from it. In Your death, I will daily live. In Your life, I will daily die. Abiding in You, may my will, through the power of Your eternal Spirit, become a finely tuned instrument which yields to every touch of the will of my God. With my whole soul, I say with You and in You. "Father! not as I will, but as Thou wilt."

Blessed Lord! Open my heart, and the hearts of all Your people, to fully take in the glory of the truth: That a will, given up to God, is a will God accepts for use in His service, to desire, determine, and will what is according to God's will. Let mine be a will which, by the power of the Holy Spirit, exercises its royal prerogative in prayer. Let it loose and bind in heaven and on earth, asking whatever it chooses, and saying it will be done.

O Lord Jesus! Teach me to pray. Amen.

CHAPTER 29:
OUR BOLDNESS IN PRAYER

"And this is the confidence that we have in him, that, if we ask any thing according to his will, he heareth us: And if we know that he hear us, whatsoever we ask, we know that we have the petitions that we desired of him" (1 John 5:14-15).

One of the greatest hindrances to believing prayer is undoubtedly this: Many don't know if what they ask is according to the will of God. As long as they are in doubt on this point, they cannot have the boldness to ask in the assurance that they will certainly receive. They soon begin to think that, once they have made known their requests and receive no answer, it is best to leave it to God to do according to His good pleasure. The words of John, "If we ask anything according to His will, He heareth us," as they understand them, make certainty as to an answer to prayer impossible, because they cannot be sure of what the will of God really may be. They think of God's will as His hidden counsel: How can man fathom the purpose of a God Who is wise in all things?

This is the very opposite of John's purpose writing this. He wanted to stir boldness and confidence in us, until we had the full assurance of faith in prayer. He says that we should have the boldness to the Father that we know we are asking according to His will, and we know that He hears us. With such boldness, He will hear us no matter what we ask for, as long as it is according to His will. In faith we should know that we have the answer. And even as we are praying, we should be able to receive what we have asked.

John supposes that when we pray, we first find if our prayers are according to the will of God. They may be according to God's will, and yet not answered at once, or without the persevering prayer of faith. It is to give us courage to persevere and to be strong in faith that He tells us we can have boldness or confidence in prayer, because if we ask anything according to His will, He hears us. It is evident that if we are uncertain whether our petitions are according to His will, we cannot have the comfort of His promise, "We know that we have the petitions which we have asked of Him."

But this is just the difficulty. More than one believer says, "I do not know if what I desire is according to the will of God. God's will is the purpose of His infinite wisdom. It is impossible for me to know whether He considers something else better for me than what I desire. He may have reasons for holding what I asked." Everyone should understand that with such thoughts the prayer of faith becomes an impossibility. There may still be a prayer of submission or of trust in God's wisdom. But there cannot be a prayer of faith.

The great mistake here is that God's children do not really believe that it is possible to know God's will. Or if they believe this, they do not take the time and trouble to find it out. What we need is to see clearly how the Father leads His waiting, teachable child to know that his petition is according to His will. Through God's holy Word-taken up and kept in the heart, the life, and the will-and through God's Holy Spirit accepted in His dwelling and leading we will learn to know that our petitions are according to His will.

First, let us consider the Word. There is a secret will of God, with which we often fear that our prayers may be at variance. But this is not the will of God that we should be concerned with in our prayers. His will as revealed in His Word should be our concern. Our notions of a secret will that makes decrees, rendering the answers to our prayers impossible, are erroneous. Childlike faith in what He is willing to do for His children simply accepts the Father's assurance that it is His will to hear prayer and to do what faith in His Word desires and accepts. In the Word, the Father has revealed in general promises the great principles of His will with His people. The child has to take the promise and apply it to the special circumstances in His life to which it has reference. Whatever he asks within the limits of that revealed will, he may confidently expect, knowing it to be according to the will of God.

In His Word, God has given us the revelation of His will. He shows us His plans for us, His people, and for the world. With the most precious promises of grace and power, He carries out these plans through His people. As faith becomes strong and bold enough to claim the fulfillment of the general promise in the special case, we may have the assurance that our prayers are heard, because they are according to God's will. Take the words of John the verse following our text as an illustration: "If any man sees his brother sinning a sin not unto death, he shall ask and God will give him life." This is the general promise. The believer who pleads on the grounds of this promise, prays according to the will of God, and John wants him to feel the boldness to know that he has the petition for which he asks.

God's will is something spiritual and must be spiritually discerned. It is not a matter of logic that we can argue about. Not every Christian has the same gift or calling. While the general will revealed in the promises is the same for everyone, each person has a specific, individual role to fulfill in God's purpose. The wisdom of the saints is in knowing the specific will of God according to the measure of grace given us, and to ask in prayer just what God has prepared and made possible for each. The Holy Spirit dwells in us to communicate this widsom. The personal application of the general promises of the Word to our specific personal needs is given to us by the leading of the Holy Spirit.

It is this union of the teaching of the Word and the Spirit that many do not understand. This causes a twofold difficulty in knowing what God's will may be. Some seek the will of God in an inner feeling or conviction, and expect the Spirit to lead them without the Word. Others seek it in the Word, without the living leading of the Holy Spirit. The two must be united. Only in the Word and in the Spirit can we know the will of God and learn to pray according to it. In the heart, the Word and Spirit must meet. Only by indwelling can we experience their teaching. The Word must abide in us; our heart and life must be under its influence daily.

The quickening of the Word by the Spirit comes from within, not from without. Only he who yields himself entirely, in his whole life, to the supremacy of the Word and the will of God can expect to discern what that Word and will permit him to ask boldly in specific cases. The same is true of the Spirit. If I desire His leading in prayer to assure me what God's will is, my whole life must be yielded to that leading. Only in this way can mind and heart become spiritual and capable of knowing God's holy will. He who through Word and Spirit lives in the will of God by doing it; will know to pray according to that will in the confidence that He hears.

If only Christians could see what incalculable harm they do themselves by thinking that because their prayer is possibly not according to God's will, they must be content without an answer. God's Word tells us that the great reason for unanswered prayer is that we do not pray right: Ye ask and receive not, because ye ask amiss." In not granting an answer, the Father tells us that there is something wrong in our praying. He wants us to discover it and confess it, and so to teach us true believing and effective prayer. He can only attain this object when He brings us to the place where we see that we are to blame for the withholding of the answer. Our aims, our faith, or our lives are not what they should be. God is frustrated as long as we are content to say "Perhaps it is because my prayer is not according to His will that He does not hear me."

O let us no longer throw the blame for our unanswered prayers on the secret will of God, but on our own faulty praying! Let that word, "Ye receive not because ye ask amiss," be a lantern of the Lord, searching heart and life to prove that we are indeed those to whom Christ gave His promises of certain answers! Let us believe that we can know if our prayers are according to God's will! Let us yield our hearts to the indwelling of the Word of the Father to have Christ's Word abiding in us. We should live day by day with the anointing that teaches all things. If we yield ourselves unreservedly to the Holy Spirit as He teaches us to abide in Christ and to dwell in the Father's presence, we will soon understand how the Father's love longs for the child to know His will. In the confidence that that will includes every thing His power and love have promised to do, we should know, too, that He hears all of our prayers. "This is the boldness which we have, that if we ask anything according to His will, He heareth us."

Lord, teach us to pray.

Blessed Master! With my whole heart I thank You for the blessed lesson that the path to a life full of answers to prayer is through the will of God. Lord! Teach me to know this blessed will by living it, loving it, and always doing it. In this way, I will learn to offer prayers according to that will. In their harmony with God's blessed will, I will find boldness in prayer and confidence in accepting the answer.

Father! It is Your will that Your child should enjoy Your presence and blessing. It is Your will that everything in Your child's life should be in accordance with Your will, and that the

234

Holy Spirit should work this in him. It is Your will that Your child should live in the daily experience of distinct answers to prayer, in order to enjoy living and direct fellowship with Yourself. It is Your will that Your Name should be glorified in and through Your children, and that it will be in those who trust You. O my Father! Let this will of Yours be my confidence in everything I ask.

Blessed Savior! Teach me to believe in the glory of this will. That will is the eternal love that, with Divine power, works out its purpose in each human will that yields itself to it. Lord! Teach me this! You can make me see how every promise and every command of the Word is indeed the will of God, and that its fulfillment is given to me by God Himself. Let His will become the sure rock on which prayer and my assurance of an answer always rest Amen.

AUTHOR'S NOTE

There is often great confusion as to the will of God. People think that what God wills must inevitably take place. This is by no means the case. God wills a great deal of blessing to His people which never comes to them. He wills it most earnestly, but they do not will it. Hence, it cannot come to them. This is the great mystery of man's creation with a free will and the renewal of his will in redemption. God has made the execution of His will dependent on the will of man. God's will as revealed in His promises will be fulfilled as much as our faith allow. Prayer is the power by which something comes to pass which otherwise would not have taken place. And faith the power which determines how much of God's will is done in us. Once God reveals to a soul what He is willing to do for it, the responsibility for the execution of that will rests with us.

Some are afraid that this is putting too much power into the hands of man. But all power is put into the hands of man through Christ Jesus (Luke 10:19). The key to prayer and all power is His. When we learn to understand that He is just as much one with us as with the Father, see how natural, right, and safe it is that such power is given. Christ the Son has the right to ask whatever I chooses. Through our abiding in Him and His abiding in us, His Spirit breathes in us what He wants to ask and obtain through us. We pray in His Name. The prayers are as much ours as they are His.

Others fear that to believe that prayer has such power limits the liberty and the love of God. O if we only knew how we are limiting His liberty and His love by not allowing Him to act in the only way in which He chooses to act, now that He has taken us up into fellowship with Himself! Our prayer is like pipes, though which water is carried from a large mountain stream to a town some distance away. Such water pipes don't make the water willing to flow down from the hills, nor do they give it its power of blessing and refreshment. This is its very nature. All they do is to determine its direction.

In the same way, the very nature of God is to love and to bless. His love longs to come down to us with its quickening and refreshing streams. But He has left it to prayer to say where the blessing is channeled. He has committed it to His believing people to bring the living water to the desert places. The will of God to bless is dependent on the will of man to say where the blessing goes.

CHAPTER 30:
THE MINISTRY OF INTERCESSION

"A holy priesthood, to offer up spiritual sacrifices, acceptable to God by Jesus Christ" (I Peter 2:5)

"Ye shall be named the Priests of the Lord." (Isaiah 61:6).

"The Spirit of the Lord God is upon me: because the Lord hath anointed me." These are the words of Jesus in Isaiah, chapter sixty-one. As the fruit of His work, all redeemed ones are priests-fellow-partakers with Him of His anointing with the Spirit as High Priest. This anointing is "Like the precious ointment upon the beard of Aaron, that went down to the skirts of his garments" (Psalm 133:2). Like every son of Aaron, every member of Jesus' Body has a right to the priesthood. But not everyone exercises it.Many are still entirely ignorant of it. And yet it is the highest privilege of a child of God, the mark of greatest nearness and likeness to Him "Whoever liveth to pray." Do you doubt this? Think of what constitutes priesthood.

There is, first, the work of the priesthood. This has two sides: one Godward, the other manward. "Every priest is ordained for men in things pertaining to God" (Hebrews 5:1). Or, as it is said by Moses (Deuteronomy 10:8, 21:5, 33:10; Malachi 2:6): "The Lord separated the tribe of Levi, to stand before the Lord to minister unto Him, and to bless His Name. " On the one hand, the priest had the power to draw nigh to God, to dwell with Him in His house, and to present Him with the blood of the sacrifice or the burning incense. This work he did not do, however, on his own behalf, but for the sake of the people whose representative he was. This is the other side of his work. He received people's sacrifices, presented them to God, and then came out to bless in His Name, giving the assurance of His favor and teaching them His law.

A priest is thus a man who does not live for himself. He lives with God and for God. His work as God's servant is to care for His house, His honor,and His worship, making known to men His love and His will. He lives with men and for men (Hebrews 5:2). His work is to find out their sins and needs, bring these before God, offer sacrifice and incense in their names, obtain forgiveness and blessing for them, and then to come out and bless them in His Name.

This is the high calling of every believer. They have been redeemed with the one purpose of being God's priests in the midst of the perishing millions around them. In conformity to Jesus, the Great High Priest, they are to be the ministers and stewards of the grace of God.

Secondly, there is the walk of the priesthood, harmony with its work. As God is holy, so the priest was to be especially holy. This means not only separated from everything unclean, but holy unto God-being set apart and given up to God for His use. Separation from the world and being given to God were indicated in many ways.

It was seen in the clothing. The holy garment made according to God's own orders, marked the priests as His (Exodus 28). It was seen in the command as to their special purity and freedom from contact with death and defilement. Much that was allowed to an ordinary Israelite was forbidden them. Priests could have no bodily defects or blemishes. Bodily perfection was to be the model wholeness and holiness in God's service. The priestly tribes were to have no inheritance with the other tribes. God was to be their inheritance. Their life was to be one of faith-set apart unto God; they were to live on Him as well as for Him. All this symbolic of what the character of the New Testament priest is to be. Our priestly power with God depends on our personal life and walk. Jesus must be able to say of our walk on earth, "They have not defiled their garments."

In our separation from the world, we must prove that our desire to be holy to the Lord is whole-hearted and entire. The bodily perfection of the priest must have its counterpart in our also being "without spot or blemish." We must be "the man of God, perfect, thoroughly furnished unto all good works," "perfect and entire, wanting nothing" (Leviticus 21:17-21; Ephesians 5:27; 2 Timothy 3:17; James 1:4). Above all, we must consent to give up all inheritance on earth. We must forsake everything and like Christ have need only of God and keep everything for Him alone. This marks the true priest, the man who only lives for God and his fellow-men.

Thirdly, there is the way to the priesthood. God had chosen all of Aaron's sons to be priests. Each of them was a priest by birth. Yet he could not begin his work without a special act of ordinance-his consecration. Every child of God is a priest by right of his birth-his blood relationship to the Great High Priest. But he can exercise his power only as he accepts and realizes his consecration.

With Aaron and his sons it took place thus (Exodus 29): After being washed and clothed, they were anointed with the holy oil. Sacrifices were then offered, and the right ear, the right hand, and the right foot were touched with the blood. They and their garments were then sprinkled with the blood and the oil together. In the same way, as the blood and the Spirit work more fully in the child of God, the power of the Holy Priesthood will also work in him. The blood will take away all sense of unworthiness; the Spirit will take away all sense of unfitness.

Notice what was new in the application of the blood to the priest. If he had ever as a penitent sought forgiveness by bringing a sacrifice for his sin, the blood was sprinkled on the altar, but not on his person. But now, for priestly consecration, there was to be closer contact with the blood. The ear, hand and foot were by a special act brought under its power, and the whole being sanctified for God. When the believer is led to seek full priestly access God, he feels the need of a fuller and more enduring experience of the power of the blood. Where he had previously been content to have the blood sprinkled only on the mercy seat as what he needed for pardon, he now needs a more personal sprinkling a cleansing of his heart from an evil conscience. Through this, he has "no more conscience of sin" (Hebrews 10:2); he is cleansed from all sin. As he gets to enjoy this, his consciousness is awakened to his wonderful right of intimate access to God, and the full assurance that his intercessions are acceptable.

As the blood gives the right, the Spirit gives the power for believing intercession. He breathes into the priestly spirit a burning love for God's honor and the saving of souls. He makes us one with Jesus to the extent that prayer in His Name is reality. The more the Christian is truly filled with the Spirit of Christ, the more spontaneous will be his giving himself up to the life of priestly intercession.

Beloved fellow-Christians! God needs priests who can draw close to Him, live in His presence, and by their intercession draw down the blessings of His grace on others. And the world needs priests who will bear the burden of the perishing ones and intercede on their behalf.

Are you willing to offer yourself for this holy work? You know the surrender it demands-nothing less than the Christ-like giving up of everything, so that the salvation of God's love may be accomplished among men. Don't be one of those who are content with being saved, just doing enough work to keep themselves warm and lively! Let nothing keep you back from giving yourselves to be wholly and only priests of the Most High God!

The thought of unworthiness or of unfitness need not keep you back. In the blood, the objective power of the perfect redemption works in you. In the Spirit, the full, subjective, personal experience of a Divine life is secured. The blood provides an infinite worthiness to make your prayers acceptable. The Spirit provides a Divine fitness, teaching you to pray exactly according to the will of God.

Every priest knew that when he presented a sacrifice according to the law of the sanctuary, it was accepted. Under the covering of the blood and the Spirit, you have the assurance that all the wonderful promises of prayer in the Name of Jesus will be fulfilled in you. Abiding in union with the Great High Priest, "You shall ask what you will, and it shall be done unto you." You will have power to pray the effective prayer of the righteous man that accomplishes a great deal. You will not only join in the general prayer of the Church for the world, but be able in your own sphere to take up your own special work in prayer. As priests, you will work on a personal basis with God to receive and know the answer, and so to bless in His Name.

Come, brother, come! Be a priest, only a priest, and all priest! Walk before the Lord in the full consciousness that you have been set apart for the holy ministry of intercession. This is the true blessedness of conformity to the image of God's Son.

Lord, teach us to pray.

O my blessed High Priest! Accept the consecration in which my soul responds to Your message! I believe in the holy priesthood of Your saints I believe that I am a priest, having the power to appear before the Father in prayer that will bring down many blessings on the perishing souls around me.

I believe in the power of Your precious blood to cleanse me from all sin. It gives me perfect confidence in God and brings me near to Him in the full assurance of faith that my intercession will be heard.

I believe in the anointing of the Spirit. It comes down to me daily from You, my Great High Priest, to sanctify me. It fills me with the consciousness my priestly calling and with the love of souls. It also teaches me what is according to God's will and how to pray the prayer of faith.

I believe that, just as You are in all things in life, You are in my prayer life, drawing me up in it the fellowship of Your wondrous work of intercession.

In this faith, I yield myself today to my God as one of His anointed priests. I stand before Him to intercede on behalf of sinners, and then return to bless them in His Name.

Holy Lord Jesus! Accept and seal my consecration. Lay Your hands on me and consecrate me Yourself to this holy work. Let me walk among men with the consciousness and the character of a priest or the Most High God.

And to Him Who loved us-Who washed us from our sins in His own blood, and Who made us kings and priests before God, His Father-to Him be glory and power forever! Amen.

CHAPTER 31:
A Life of Prayer

"Rejoice evermore. Pray without ceasing. In everything give thanks" (I Thessalonians 5:16-18).

Our Lord told the parable of the widow and the unjust judge to teach us that men ought to pray without ceasing. The widow persevered in seeking one definite thing. The parable appears to refer to persevering in prayer for some special blessing, when God delays or appears to refuse. The Epistles, which speak of continuing in prayer, watching for the answer, and praying always in the Spirit, appear to refer to something different-the whole life being one of prayer. As the soul longs for the manifestation of God's glory to us, in us, through us, and around us, the inmost life of the soul is continually rising upward in dependence, faith, longing desire, and trustful expectation.

What is needed to live such a life of prayer? The first thing is undoubtedly an entire sacrifice of one's life to God's Kingdom and glory. If you try to pray without ceasing because you want to be very pious and good, you will never succeed. Yielding ourselves to live for God and His honor enlarges the heart and teaches us to regard everything in the light of God and His will. We instinctively recognize in everything around us the need for God's help and blessing, and an opportunity for His being glorified.

Everything is weighed and tested by the one thing that fills the heart: the glory of God. The soul has learned that only what is of God can really glorify Him. Through the heart and soul, the whole life becomes a looking up, a crying from the inmost heart, for God to prove His power and love, and reveal His glory. The believer awakes to the consciousness that he is one of the watchmen on Zion's walls, whose call really does touch and move the King in heaven to do what would otherwise not be done. He understands how real Paul's exhortation was: "praying always with all prayer and supplication in the Spirit for all the saints and for me," and "continue in prayer, with all praying also for us." To forget oneself-to live for God and His Kingdom among men-is the way to learn to pray without ceasing.

This life devoted to God must be accompanied by the deep confidence that our prayer is effective. In His prayer lessons, our Blessed Lord insisted on faith in the Father as a God Who most certainly does what we ask. "Ask and ye shall receive." To count confidently on an answer is the beginning and the end of His teaching. (Compare Matthew 7:8 and John 16:24.)

As we gain the assurance that our prayers are effective and that God does what we ask, we dare not neglect the use of this wonderful power. Our souls should turn wholly to God, and our lives should become prayer. The Lord needs and takes time, because we and everyone around us are creatures of time, subject to the law of growth. But know that not one single prayer of faith can possibly be lost, and that sometimes there is a necessity for accumulating prayer. Know that persevering prayer pleases God. Prayer becomes the quiet, persistent living of our life of desire and faith in the presence of our God.

Don't limit such free and sure promises of the living God with your reasoning any longer! Don't rob them of their power, and ourselves of the wonderful confidence they are meant to inspire! The hindrance is not in God, not in His secret will, and not in the limitations of His promises. It is in us. We are not what we should be to obtain the promise. Open your whole heart to God's words of promise in all their simplicity and truth! They will search us and humble us. They will lift us up and make us glad and strong. To the faith that knows it gets what it asks for, prayer is not a work or a burden, but a joy and a triumph. It becomes a necessity and a second nature.

This union of strong desire and firm confidence is nothing but the life of the Holy Spirit within us. The Holy Spirit dwells in us, hides Himself in the depths of our being, and stirs our desire for the Unseen and the Divine-God Himself. It is always the Holy Spirit Who draws out the heart to thirst for God and to long for His being recognized and glorified. Sometimes He speaks through us in groanings that cannot be uttered, sometimes in clear and conscious assurance, sometimes in distinct petitions for the deeper revelation of Christ to ourselves, and sometimes in pleas for a soul, a work, the Church or the world. Where the child of God really lives and walks in the Spirit-where he is not content to remain carnal, but tries to be a fit, spiritual organ for the Divine Spirit to reveal the life of Christ and Christ Himself-there the neverceasing life of intercession of the Blessed Son must reveal and repeat itself. Because it is the Spirit of Christ Who prays in us, our prayers must be heard. Because it is we who pray in the Spirit, there is need of time, patience, and continual renewing of the prayer until every obstacle is conquered, and the harmony between God's Spirit and ours is perfect.

The chief thing we need for a life of unceasing prayer is to know that Jesus teaches us to pray. We have begun to understand a little of what His teaching is. It isn't the communication of new thoughts or views, the discovery of failure or error, nor the arousal of desire and faith, however important all this may be. Jesus' teaching takes us up into the fellowship of His own prayer-life before the Father. This is how Jesus really teaches. It was the sight of Jesus praying that made the disciples ask to be taught to pray. The faith of Jesus' continuous prayer truly teaches us to pray.

We know why: He Who prays is our Head and our life. All He has is ours and is given to us when we give ourselves completely to Him. By His blood, He leads us into the immediate presence of God. The inner sanctuary is our home; we live there. Living so close to God and knowing we have been taken there to bless those who are far away, we cannot help but pray.

Christ makes us partakers with Himself of His prayer-power and prayer-life. Our true aim must not be to work a great deal and pray just enough to keep the work right. We should pray a great deal and then work enough for the power and blessing obtained in prayer to find its way through us to men. Christ lives to pray eternally; He saves and reigns. He communicates His prayer-life to us and maintains it in us if we trust Him. He is responsible for our praying without ceasing. Christ teaches us to pray by showing us how He does it, by doing it in us, and by leading us to do it in Him and like Him. Christ is everything-the life and the strength-for a neverceasing prayer-life. Seeing Christ's continuous praying as our life enables us to pray without ceasing. Because His priesthood is the power of an endless life-that resurrection life that never fades and never fails-and because His life is our life, praying without ceasing can become the joy of heaven here on earth. The Apostle says, "Rejoice evermore: pray without ceasing: in everything give thanks." Supported by never-ceasing joy and neverceasing praise, never-ceasing prayer is the manifestation of the power of the eternal life where Jesus always prays.

The union between the Vine and the branch is indeed a prayer union. The highest conformity to Christ-the most blessed participation in the glory of His heavenly life-is that we take part in His work of intercession. He and we live forever to pray. In union with Him, praying without ceasing becomes a possibility-a reality, the holiest and most blessed part of our holy and blessed fellowship with God. We abide within the veil in the presence of the Father. What the Father says, we do. What the Son asks, the Father does. Praying without ceasing is the earthly manifestation of heaven, a foretaste of the life where they rest neither day nor night in their song of worship and adoration.

Lord, teach us to pray.

O my Father! With my whole heart I praise You for this wondrous life of continuous prayer, continuous fellowship, continuous answers, and continuous oneness with Him Who lives to pray forever! O my God! Keep me abiding and walking in the presence of Your glory, so that prayer may be the spontaneous expression of my life with You.

Blessed Savior! With my whole heart I praise You for coming from heaven to share my needs and my pleas, so that I could share Your all- powerful intercession. Thank You for taking me into Your school of prayer, teaching me the blessedness and the power of a life that is totally comprised of prayer. And most of all, thank You for taking me up into the fellowship of Your life of intercession. Now through me, too, Your blessings can be dispensed to those around me.

Holy Spirit! With deep reverence I thank You for Your work in me. Through You I am lifted up into communication with the Son and the Father, entering the fellowship of the life and love of the Holy Trinity.

Spirit of God! Perfect Your work in me! Bring me into perfect union with Christ, My Intercessor! Let Your unceasing indwelling make my life one of unceasing intercession. And let my life unceasingly glorify the Father and bless those around me. Amen.

Made in the USA
Las Vegas, NV
28 July 2021

27125335R00148